Cashing the Prevention Check

Cashing the Prevention Check

✦

An Executive Guide to Leading an Organization to Prevention

Larry McFadin with Beeler Gausz

iUniverse, Inc.

New York Lincoln Shanghai

Cashing the Prevention Check
An Executive Guide to Leading an Organization to Prevention

iUniverse books may be ordered through booksellers or by contacting:

iUniverse
2021 Pine Lake Road, Suite 100
Lincoln, NE 68512
www.iuniverse.com
1-800-Authors (1-800-288-4677)

ISBN-13: 978-0-595-35973-8 (pbk)
ISBN-13: 978-0-595-67304-9 (cloth)
ISBN-13: 978-0-595-80423-8 (ebk)
ISBN-10: 0-595-35973-6 (pbk)
ISBN-10: 0-595-67304-X (cloth)
ISBN-10: 0-595-80423-3 (ebk)

Printed in the United States of America

Contents

Acknowledgments

I have been working on the ideas in this book since my early days at Ling-Temco-Vought Aerospace Corporation in the late 1960s. I am, by nature, a note taker and collector of material that I might want to recall at a later date. During these last forty years, I have written articles, given speeches, and consulted with clients all over the globe. I owe a debt of gratitude to my clients, who have given me a great education and provided me with lessons learned and material accumulated in this book.

Every once in a while, I accumulate notes on similar subjects into folders. In the beginning, these notes were unorganized, but from time to time I reviewed them and did a rough organization of the material. Of course, since the material was written at different times from different mind-sets, the organization was really rough. Several times I had decided to use this material to write a book. After a few days of working, however—trying to make it sound like it came from the same author on a single subject—I had given up and gone on to the day-to-day activities that consume our time.

Beeler Gausz is a colleague at the Ion Group. The Ion Group is a consulting firm that helps organizations eliminate mistakes, errors, and defects. He and I have worked together for many of the last twenty years. Last December, we were in Tokyo on a consulting assignment, and one evening before dinner he asked why I had not written a book about what we do. I explained that I had always intended to do so but just could not do what it would take to make a book out of the materials I had organized. He offered to help me write it.

"Beeler," I said, "you do not know what you are getting into. You need to look at what I have before you decide to get involved in such an undertaking. The ideas are there, but the presentation is really rough. It will take a lot of work."

"OK. I want to help. Let me look at it," he countered.

I flipped open the laptop and opened the Improvement Book folder. "There it is. Take your time and look carefully. I'll go down to the bar and wait. You can come down when you finish and let me know what you think." With that, I left the room and went down to the bar.

A couple of hours later, Beeler appeared at the restaurant. He did not look discouraged. As a matter of fact, he looked positive. "I went over a lot of it. I think we can do it!" he said.

"Are you sure?" I asked.

"Yes, it'll be fun," he said.

I agreed and gave him a copy of the Improvement Folder. We set a time for the first meeting to review the effort and began work on the book.

Needless to say, the book would not have been published without Beeler's help and counsel. I want to thank him for his encouragement and efforts.

When Beeler and I finished the book, we turned it over to my wife, Judy. She read it to see if it fit together, and she also provided editing and formatting.

I owe a lot to both of them for their efforts in helping to publish *Cashing the Prevention Check*.

1

The Need for Prevention

The need for performance improvement is perpetual. If any-thing in business is relentless, it is that things go wrong. A typi-cal business wastes 30 percent of its operating costs fixing things that have gone bad.

As an introduction to the book, let me share a story about Juan and Rita Rivera. They are engaged in a relatively simple transaction: buying a condominium.

The Casa Solana Case

Juan and Rita Rivera had driven from Orlando to Atlanta to do a walk-through of the condo for which they had signed a contract a month earlier. They were eager to see the condo with their requested upgrades installed. They had opted for granite coun-tertops in the kitchen and baths, wood floors in all rooms except the bedrooms, upgraded carpets in the bedrooms, and upgraded stainless-steel appliances. A previously scheduled walk-through had been postponed by the seller two weeks before.

Juan and Rita arrived at the condo sales office a few minutes early, and were greeted by the staff.

"I hope you had a nice drive up. We're ready for your walk-through. We'll touch-up any problems you find during the walk-through, and we're on schedule for the closing next Mon-day as planned. Sandra will be with you in a few minutes. Please

1

help yourselves to coffee or a soft drink," Melissa offered. "You know where they are."

"Yes, we do, Melissa, thank you," Rita responded.

In the refreshment area, Rita said, "It's nice to work with these young people—they're always friendly and upbeat."

"Yes," Juan agreed. "They make you feel welcome."

Just as they were finishing their coffee, Sandra entered. "Good morning, Mr. and Mrs. Rivera. Hope you had a nice trip up from Orlando. I walked through the condo yesterday, and things look good. I had them put a little paint in a place or two, but everything else is ready for you. We'll have a punch-list guy with us, and he'll touch up things as we go," Sandra explained.

"Just for your information, Cameron, your sales associate, is no longer with us—she's gone on to other things," she continued. "I'll be handling your account now."

Rita and Juan nodded their understanding.

"Before we go, I want to discuss the preliminary closing statement you sent us," Juan said. "We've already paid $10,114 for the upgrades, but that's not shown on the statement. The money due to the seller at closing should be $10,114 less."

Sandra said, "Melissa will look into that while we do the walk-through, and she'll have an answer by the time we finish."

Sandra picked up a checklist on which to note any items that needed to be corrected before the close. She entered the security code and opened the door to the condo.

Juan and Rita immediately noticed the wood floors. They looked great!

Then Juan walked toward the kitchen. "The appliances are not stainless-steel," he observed. "We were supposed to be upgraded to stainless appliances."

Sandra said, "That's not a problem—we'll get them changed out tomorrow."

Rita ran her fingers over the granite countertop in the kitchen. "Looks good!" she exclaimed.

Rita then went into the master bedroom, where she noticed that the carpets had not been changed. "We were supposed to have been upgraded to Berber," she said.

Sandra countered, "That was not on the upgrade list."

Juan said, "We paid $10,000 for upgrades, and that was part of the package."

The touch-up technician looked at Sandra and said, "The Berber is part of a full upgrade package."

Sandra agreed.

As they continued the walk-through, Juan and Rita discovered that only one of the two bathroom counters had been upgraded. Sandra had had enough. "We need to go back to the office and get this upgrade matter cleared up."

Back at the office, Sandra pulled the sales folder for the condo unit, and sure enough, the paperwork indicated that Juan and Rita had indeed purchased the complete upgrade package. Sandra handed Juan the walk-through checklist and said, "I'll give you a vendor key so you can return to the unit and can take your time walking through. Please check everything and note anything you find that you feel needs to be fixed. I'll stay here and begin to contact the vendors to get this resolved quickly." She told the touch-up technician that he would not be needed until Rita and Juan had completed the walk-through.

While the Riveras returned to inspect the condo, Melissa found, in the Riveras' file, copies of the checks they had written for the upgrades. Evidently, the closing attorney had not been informed of these upgrades. Sandra would assure the Riveras that the final closing statement would reflect the correct amount.

The Riveras returned to the condo unit and conducted a thorough walk-through. They noted seven relatively minor issues that needed to be resolved and returned to the sales office to discuss their problems and what impact they would have on the closing date.

Everyone agreed that the developer would work over the weekend to get everything repaired and replaced—with the exception of one piece of granite that had been ordered and would not be delivered until later—and that the condo would be ready for a final walk-through on the next Monday, the day originally scheduled for closing. The delay in the granite delivery would require the postponement of the closing until after the installation of the granite.

An additional issue, Sandra noted, was that the original closing attorney would be unavailable after the original closing date. The condo developer would have to find another closing attorney.

The Riveras were not happy about this, but they did not make a scene.

Outside the office, Rita said, "This'll cost us another trip and more missed time at work. What should have been fun has turned into a chore."

Juan agreed.

Monday was a cool morning as Juan and Rita arrived at the sales office. They were excited to at last see their completed condo before they returned to Orlando, but disappointed that the closing would not be taking place this morning.

"Good morning," Melissa greeted them as they entered. "Sandra will be right with you."

Sandra arrived momentarily. "Melissa will go on the walk-through with you this morning. I think we're ready except for that one piece of granite."

They proceeded to the unit, but inside they observed that only three of the seven problems that had been noted had been resolved. They returned to the sales office to complain, and another walk-through was promised. They were introduced to the new closing attorney, who assured them he would redo the closing statement to reflect the accurate closing numbers.

Juan and Rita returned to Orlando once more, to again await a phone call to schedule the final walk-through and closing.

And after yet more difficulties, Juan and Rita finally moved into their condo…several weeks later.

Bad things happen unless there is a commitment to taking actions to keep them from happening. Fixing things after they have gone wrong is not good enough. Every part of the organization must work toward prevention. Everything done in the organization must be done with prevention in mind.

The Casa Solana case provides a simple, yet real world example, of a situation that has gone wrong. In this case, no one is happy with the way the transaction progressed. Disputes are resolved, but the resolution cost both emotional and financial resources. Such situations do not have to happen. There is another way. In the remainder of the book, we will investigate the steps that can be taken by an organization to prevent disappointing events from occurring. Eliminating these disappointments will save not only time and money but also emotional distress.

We live in a world where things do not always go as planned. This is true even though we have endured decades of learning and applying quality and productivity management in virtually everything we do. After all this effort to improve, there is still virtually no business endeavor in which things always go right. In the more than thirty years I have spent helping organizations improve, I have learned that businesses continue to waste roughly 30 percent of their operating expenses to make up for things that go wrong. The things that go wrong are referred to by many names, but most frequently are referred to as mistakes, errors, and defects. In order to simplify things, I will refer to all of these as MEDs, short for "Mistakes, Errors, and Defects." Regardless of what they are called, they are all the result of doing something incorrectly or not according to plan. They could also be the result of incorrect or inadequate planning from the very beginning. Whatever the reason, MEDs result in a shortfall in expected performance. Thirty percent! That's significantly greater than a typical business's profits. It's a substantial amount of money to forfeit because things go wrong.

Business organizations are not alone. It doesn't seem to matter whether the endeavor is related to national defense, to health and safety, or to a simple task like doing laundry, mowing yards, or painting doors. Things go wrong. The MEDs can be part of a massive undertaking involving hundreds of people or part of a simple activity such as an individual voting in a voting booth. Things go wrong. Some things go wrong over a long period of time, while other things go bad in a fraction of a second. But in the final analysis, regardless of the circumstance, a MED occurred.

We find MEDs everywhere we look. Even in sectors of society that place a priority on safety—such as airlines, hospitals, space exploration, and the military—MEDs occur. Airplanes miss schedules and worse. Doctors and hospitals make MEDs from diagnosis to surgery. X-rays are misread; prescriptions are incorrectly administered. Space vehicles destruct during liftoff, miss targets, and fail to respond after launch. Smart bombs miss their targets, and soldiers are killed by friendly fire. Regardless of oaths to quality and good intentions, the routine existence of MEDs remains commonplace. The results are costly, disappointing, and sometimes catastrophic.

There are MEDs in the insurance and banking industries, at Internet service providers, auto and computer manufacturers, local grocery stores, credit card companies, and neighborhood service providers. The impression is that little happens as we expect it should unless and until we complain. It takes a squeaking wheel to get the grease. If you need more proof, pick up the newspaper or watch the news on television.

Some argue that life is so complex that things must go wrong. Yet even simple tasks are frequently not done correctly. Invoices contain erroneous information or arrive late. Documents are misfiled or lost.

Mail is delivered to the wrong address. Managers fail to communicate with everyone involved in key business transactions. The list seems endless.

Still others argue that the reason things will always go wrong is due to some natural law. Work processes decay or fall apart a little at a time until the outcome of the process is totally unpredictable. These same people argue that these processes must be continuously propped up to keep it going. This natural decay is easily seen in manufacturing processes, but the tendencies are just as true and unforgiving in service industry processes. The questions are "Why?" and "What causes this decay?" Is the fact that things go wrong something people have to accept as inevitable, or is it possible that people can cause work processes to go right instead of wrong?

What is needed is an organizational approach that anticipates and prevents problems rather than an approach that reacts to things after they have already gone wrong. This needed approach is based on prevention rather than fixing. Prevention is not only possible but also quite practical.

The weight of experience shows that MEDs can be prevented. Some believe that prevention is impossible. Nothing could be further from the truth. The good news is that, over time, all types of organizations have proven it possible to make things go right; some have made it the norm rather than the exception. To make this happen, however, requires commitment and hard work.

Many organizations have been trying unsuccessfully to deal with MEDs for many years. This lack of success has generally been caused by implementing the wrong solution. A common solution is to attempt to mollify disgruntled customers after a problem has occurred. In many of these cases, organizations install systems that somehow compensate the customer who has experienced a MED. Still others spend an excess of money on improvement technology without properly addressing the culture of the users of that technology. In these instances, MEDs continue. MEDs continue in spite of the platitudes uttered by management. As a result, commitments waiver, and the individuals that constitute the organization become more and more skeptical. It is imperative that the approach chosen to prevent MEDs be based on sound, proven principles.

The roads chosen by conscientious organizations are as varied as the results they have achieved. Most organizations try a variety of schemes to improve. The approaches organizations select involve everything from coordinated, enterprise-wide initiatives to isolated efforts involving only portions of the organization. Some businesses have progressively built a layered improvement approach and have integrated improvement into the day-to-day way of doing business. Others commission individual soldiers or entire armies of problem fighters who are dispatched to eliminate problems as they are found.

Those that have institutionalized and integrated their improvement efforts into their day-to-day operations continue to benefit from a culture of improvement. Their organizations have made significant, unprecedented, and tangible bottom-line improvements in every facet of their operation. Unfortunately, others have made fitful attempts at improvement that do little more than turn the organization into a group of veteran skeptics.

The breadth of these experiences has provided a wealth of outcomes and lessons learned, especially for someone like myself who has had the good fortune to work with hundreds of different companies, government agencies, and organizations around the world. As a management consultant for nearly thirty years, I may not have seen it all, but I have seen a lot of different approaches, including all their labels, names, terminologies, egos, strengths, and weaknesses. I have seen their births and, sadly, their deaths. I have reached the conclusion that the only real approach to organizational performance improvement is that which results in the prevention of MEDs. Anything else is suspect. Unless we face this challenge and learn how to prevent MEDs, our organizations are at great risk.

Whenever the discussion turns to performance improvement, results are the name of the game. Without results, talk is cheap, and careers are frequently short. Good intentions are admirable, but the only rewards for just trying are those invented by the improvement aficionados themselves. It is likely these people have never had to face a meeting of stockholders. Tangible results, however, sell themselves, fuel further improvements, and result in making performance improvement a sound and perpetual effort.

Without real results, performance is left to be explained by clever accounting practices, spin doctors, and apologists. The practice of following the results of improvements to the bottom line is frequently not done. Instead, specific improvements are touted, but nothing really gets better. Cycle time stays the same, expenses remain unchanged, customer satisfaction is static, and profits do not improve.

Management should expect, as stockholders do, improvement efforts to produce demonstrated results—not just good stories with happy endings. I believe that initiating a true prevention-based improvement process is the best way to produce tangible bottom-line results, and it can happen in months, not years. Only through a prevention-based process can an organization really become better, and only then can you cash the prevention check.

My experience in helping organizations improve has convinced me that the most successful efforts take into account some very basic ingredients, which for clarity's sake can be portrayed as components of a ladder. I call it the Prevention Ladder. It provides leaders with a graphic representation of a true prevention-implementation strategy, regardless of the kind of organization they lead.

The Prevention Ladder has a universal application. The concepts and techniques embedded in the Prevention Ladder are applicable to both people and processes and are not limited by geography or cultural sensitivities. Neither does the Prevention Ladder offend anyone by favoring one guru over another, nor does it deny an organization the use of valuable improvement techniques just because it is not certified by the appropriate cult leader. The Prevention Ladder provides a template that shows how to improve any organization's performance by doing things to make prevention a reality. But this can only happen if an organization's management develops a habitual focus on prevention.

The remainder of this book will provide a detailed description of the Prevention Ladder. The intention of this book is to provide a guide for executives who want to successfully lead their organization's prevention activities. As we move through the material, please remember that every ladder is constructed from simple but equally necessary components: two vertical rails and a number of horizontal rungs. Each rung must be firmly attached to both rails in order to make it serviceable and safe. The Prevention Ladder shares those same strategic characteristics. Now is the time to share it with you.

2

Prevention: The Key to Improvement

There is only one way to do things right, and that is not to do things wrong. The more often you do not do things wrong, the more often you realize that doing things right all the time isn't that difficult, and is, by the way, what you should have been doing anyway.

It is interesting to talk to executives today about the subject of improved organizational performance. Typically, they're not interested and react with a "been there, done that" look on their faces. Most still have corrective teams working on some projects and a team of black belts at the ready for the next round of problems. Yet when the subject of discussion changes to things that go wrong in their organizations, there is plenty to talk about. I believe they're routinely living with MEDs now because their past improvement initiatives were too narrow in scope. In many cases the improvement initiatives were delegated to their employees when they should have been handled by management, or the concepts and tools offered in the initiative selected were too limited. It seems that everyone is for improvement as long as it's simple and as long as they themselves do not have to be involved to any great extent. This executive bent on simplicity and minor personal involvement has been a major reason for the lack of a significant reduction in the number of MEDs.

As a result, the organizational improvers of the 1980s and 1990s dutifully tackled organizations with mathematical and logic-based approaches in an attempt to make things better. The last twenty-five years have left a trail of approaches such as quality circles, statistical quality control, quality management, reengineering, and Six Sigma programs. There is certainly nothing wrong with these efforts, unless management believes that they are the full extent of what must be done to make an organization better. The idea that a simple approach by the rank and file that utilizes five tools, seven tools, or even twenty tools can change an organization into one that routinely prevents real problems is a problem itself. The idea of prevention is in itself simple and easy to understand—just keep MEDs from happening. Making this idea a habit in every part of the organization is, however, another issue.

To move forward, and we must, it is not necessary to accept perfection as the standard of performance; it is, however, necessary to understand and commit to preventing the things that should not happen from happening. One begins this journey by understanding the concept of prevention. During the journey, you will see the incredibly positive power that prevention has on organizational performance.

The story of prevention begins at the lowest level of doing things, whether the activity in question is writing a report, communicating with an associate, manufacturing a part, or making a decision. It always also involves people. When we properly take care of the details of everything we do and properly take care of all the people involved, we are on our way to preventing. Following this basic approach quickly adds up to improvement of overall organizational performance.

Taking care of the details of everything we do and taking care of all the people involved is simple in concept but can quickly lead to the suspicion that things will be micromanaged, time will be wasted, and nothing will move forward. In fact, these feelings and notions are nothing more than reactions to the contrast between true prevention and the way we usually steer an organization. What we must do is create an organization that habitually acts to provide its people with the wherewithal to individually manage his or her own work processes. The objective is to develop associates who have the capability to know what to do routinely to cause prevention and who are enthusiastic about the opportunity to help prevent. The objective of developing associates who enthusiastically prevent is the key to instituting the behavioral characteristics we are looking for. As this capability develops, it signals that the organization is transforming into a prevention-oriented one.

There are few organizations that do things right every time, all the time, but there are some that are significantly better at this than others. Think about how airplanes take off from the runways of busy airports, televisions respond to the push of a button on a remote control, the water bill arrives in the mail every month. Why do these things happen with such regularity and predictability? Is it the result of magic? Is it chance? The answer is that these processes have been structured to eliminate most of the mechanisms that cause MEDs.

Over the years, analyses of MEDs show that their root causes fall into two categories. MEDs are caused by the way the work process is defined or by the way the process is performed (or a combination of both). There is a common factor in both causes: people. People plan and implement processes, and people operate or manage processes. It is apparent that people are the key to keeping MEDs from occurring. Therefore, if we are to prevent MEDs, we must deal with the human side of the issue as well as the process side. It is through individuals that actions must be taken to prevent MEDs.

Since MEDs are the result of two general causes, it is possible for organizations to formulate actions that keep unpleasant events from occurring in the first place. We will refer to this "keeping unpleasant or undesired events from happening" as prevention. Actions taken to cause prevention make things easier by saving money, time, emotional distress, and reputation.

If we are to prevent, we must understand that everything we do can be thought of as a series of actions or steps. This series of actions or steps defines a process. This process definition makes it clear what has to be done to produce the desired work product, and every process, of course, involves people. Any preventive action must address these two basic ingredients of processes: the work process itself and the person who manages it. Together, the process and the person create either an expected result or an unexpected result. The fact is that the organization's management decides which it will be.

In order to lean more toward expected results than unexpected ones, we know that the better the processes are defined, the more able process managers are to achieve the desired work output. It is, after all, a matter of understanding. Process definition is always the first step toward prevention, and yet it is frequently one of the least disciplined activities in an organization. The ISO 9000 series of quality standards focuses on the value of process definition. The initial efforts organizations make toward ISO 9000 certification are directly related to defining their work processes. Once defined, process definitions should not wait for review and updates from the next certification audit; they must be continually maintained. Keeping process definitions current provides the foundation for prevention.

The people closest to the work being done must manage well-defined processes. We may call these people many different names: managers, doers, operators, agents, process workers, employees, executives, or associates. But from a prevention point of view, we must think of them as process managers. They are managers because their job is to observe and monitor processes and to take appropriate action based on what they see. In many instances, they are not actually "working" the process, but they have been assigned the responsibility of managing it.

The farther removed the process manager is from the process, the less opportunity there is for prevention to happen. This is because of the physical distance or time between an occurrence or iteration of the process and the source of action necessary to control it. This is one of the truths of implementing preventive processes. The closer the controlling or managing element is to the process, the better the preventive leverage. All too often, the people closest to the process are left to flounder or to create more waste while they wait for a remote manager or action resource to notice and understand the situation, decide if action is needed, and finally define and authorize or take an action. Such situations automatically make the tasks of everyone involved corrective in nature, never preventive.

A frequent question at this point is: Where does the time and money come from to put prevention in place? The answer is simple: They come from getting results. The resources to prevent become readily available by reducing the things that go wrong and then following the time and resources saved to the bottom line. We call getting the results of prevention Planned Preventive Performance. Prevention does not task the organization with doing all new things, but it does involve getting the organization to do things differently using the proper prevention knowledge and skills. In short, people must change the way they relate to their work processes. They must move from the position of problem solving and fixing to the position of problem anticipation and prevention. Much of it is perspective. Some of it is passion. All of it is productive. All of it requires leadership.

To convert an organization of master problem solvers into a preventive organization requires bold leadership. The leader of prevention is one who understands and stands up for the incredible value of doing things right, instead of one who follows the simpler track of trailing along to pick up the remains left behind from things having been done wrong. The Prevention Ladder provides the guide for leading a preventive organization and making prevention real.

Before we explore the Ladder, I would like to share the event that started my search for a better understanding of how to make prevention a reality.

The Birth of the Prevention Ladder

During the 1980s and early 1990s, Philip Crosby Associates operated the Quality College in Winter Park, Florida. In a typical week more than a dozen classes were held at that location. In the mid-1980s, I taught one such class made up entirely of senior executives from General Motors. During the first morning of each class we would teach Philip Crosby's Four Absolutes of Quality, one of which is the concept of prevention. In this part of the class, the students would make a list of various things that could help prevent MEDs. The typical list would usually include such items as "brushing teeth," "the arm that lowers when a train approaches a crossing," and "wearing a seat belt." Toward the end of this session, I frequently would provide an example of a technique that I used to prevent me from locking myself out of my automobile: I would take two sets of keys from my pocket, hold them before the class, and explain that when I locked one set of keys in the car, I always had another set to retrieve the one left in the car. The students would usually nod or ask why I was so absentminded that I locked them in the car in the first place; but whatever the reaction of each class, there was always someone who appreciated this prevention technique. As the students in one particular class filed out of the room for a break, one of them, the vice president of quality and reliability for GM, approached the lectern.

"Larry, I realize that you do prevent locking yourself out of the car with that technique," he said, "but true prevention would be not locking the keys in the car in the first place."

I agreed with him and told him so, but again I pointed out that prevention has to have an objective (not locking myself out of the car) and that my technique was effective. I conceded that my technique involved redundancy—a second set of keys—and was, therefore, more costly than if I had prevented leaving the keys in the car to begin with. He nodded his agreement and exited the room.

I did not like the answer I had offered. As a matter of fact, I was very troubled by it. I knew he was right, and I knew that I did not have a better answer. This exchange started me thinking about true prevention. There had to be a better way to explain true prevention in the future.

The more I thought about prevention, the more I realized that it was the only Absolute of the four that I could not spend at least a day teaching, offering examples of, and leading in-depth discussions about. I realized that I understood the other three Absolutes in much greater depth than I did prevention. I also realized that this was the first time in hundreds of classes that anyone had challenged my shallow knowledge of what pre-vention really was, and it occurred to me that I was not alone in the shallow understanding of prevention. At the time, we had more than fifty executive trainers and consultants in Philip Crosby Associates. I had helped qualify many of them to teach this same subject, and none of them had challenged my under-standing of prevention either. The examples of "a stitch in time saves nine," "an ounce of prevention beats a pound of cure," and "you can pay me now or you can pay me later" had worked just fine. At least they had up until that moment.

Over the next several months, I gathered examples of every technique I could recall, observe, or imagine that related to pre-venting something bad from happening. As these examples of preventive techniques came to mind, I would list them on slips of paper and file them away. I did not review these files for the entire period of example collection, because I did not want to get into the same place in my mind where I had been when I jot-ted down the examples originally. As you would expect, there were many redundancies on the various lists, but many had new items that had never been noted before. By the end of the data-collection period, I took all the lists from the folder, cut each into pieces, one idea to a piece. The resulting piles were not pretty; there were various sizes of paper, note cards, boarding passes, and bar napkins.

I then began the process of reviewing and organizing the examples and weeding out the redundancies—the ones that weren't very good and the ones that couldn't be read. Many of the items were just industry-specific applications of a general idea or technique. At the end of this process, I had more than seven hundred separate examples of preventive actions.

The next task was to recognize any patterns that might exist within these various methods of preventing, and slowly the stacks began to show one. From this study I developed a model of prevention, which was completed several years ago. After that time, I would no longer have to rely on the stitch in time, the ounce of prevention, or the two-car key story for the explanation of prevention.

Since that time I have continued to change, evolve, refine, and expand the model.

3

The Prevention Ladder

Management must support improvement activity from a position of knowledge and expertise. It is not a game of cheerleading.

Philip Crosby, best known for inventing the concept of Zero Defects, once said, "The product of management is an organization that can do anything." As is often the case, we did not understand the full meaning of his pronouncement at the time he first said it. This statement initially set off a flurry of counterpoints asking whether management itself even had a product or not; if so, it could not be just anything. On and on the discussions went! I figured what Phil meant was that the leaders of the organization decide its destination, whatever it is, and then management makes the decisions that provide the wherewithal and willingness for the organization to achieve that goal. Managers do not simply influence performance; they cause it. They must cause the organization to move toward the desired destination. To paraphrase Phil, an organization that achieves its destination is the product of proper management.

In today's competitive marketplace, maintaining the status quo is not an option. If you pause or hesitate, you will become a casualty of the fray. To survive, every organization must strive to get better. If the organization is a product of management, as Phil said, management must know how to move the organization toward improving. This is a huge responsibility and places a large demand on management's knowledge and skill in implementing performance improvement. Once management has the knowledge and skill, it then has to convert that knowledge and skill into a plan and actions to achieve the improvement desired. In my mind, performance improvement becomes management's methodology for linking strategy with tactics. By necessity, the plan to improve organizational performance is a change plan. It changes the way organizations behave.

The knowledge and actions needed to lead a preventive organization are depicted by a ladder. Every dependable ladder has two vertical rails that support horizontal rungs. The Prevention Ladder has two rails and ten rungs. Each of these components is intended to show a part of the required knowledge and actions. An organization that is competent in prevention improvement requires everyone to become competent in two fundamental areas of knowledge:

1.   The knowledge to create error-free *processes*

2.   The knowledge to create an error-free *culture*

Both knowledge bases are fundamental to prevention and therefore, form the vertical, supporting rails of the Prevention Ladder.

The left rail deals with a fundamental knowledge that involves processes. It deals with such topics as process definition, process control, mistake proofing, and corrective action. The right rail deals with such topics as organizational behavior, communication, teamwork, and culture.

The reason these two knowledge bases are important is because past experience clearly demonstrates that organizational performance is not entirely the result of either process technology or happy, involved workers. Many organizations have tried to improve processes with little emphasis on the social or cultural aspects of the group, or they have done the opposite by focusing improvement efforts on the people side while providing little on the process side. To create a robust preventive organization, both aspects must be the focus of the performance-improvement strategy. Executives today cannot ignore the necessity of having a balanced plan and cannot make the mistake of leaving the management of improvement to either those steeped in process improvement or to those focused on organizational development. During the journey to establish a truly preventive organization, everyone's personal knowledge and proficiency in both knowledge bases will be tested.

On the Prevention Ladder, ten horizontal rungs connect both rails, and each rung represents a group of organizational-specific actions that an organization must take in order to implement prevention. Each of the ten rungs has a specific purpose in leading an organization to prevention. The actions within each rung are supported and justified by the knowledge in the rails. The actions within the rungs comprise the change plan. This plan provides the details necessary to coordinate and manage the implementation efforts. Even though I have chosen a ladder to illustrate this model, do not infer that sequential implementation of the actions defined in the rungs is necessary. The actions contained in the rungs should be ongoing and should be occurring at the same time. A diagram of the Prevention Ladder follows.

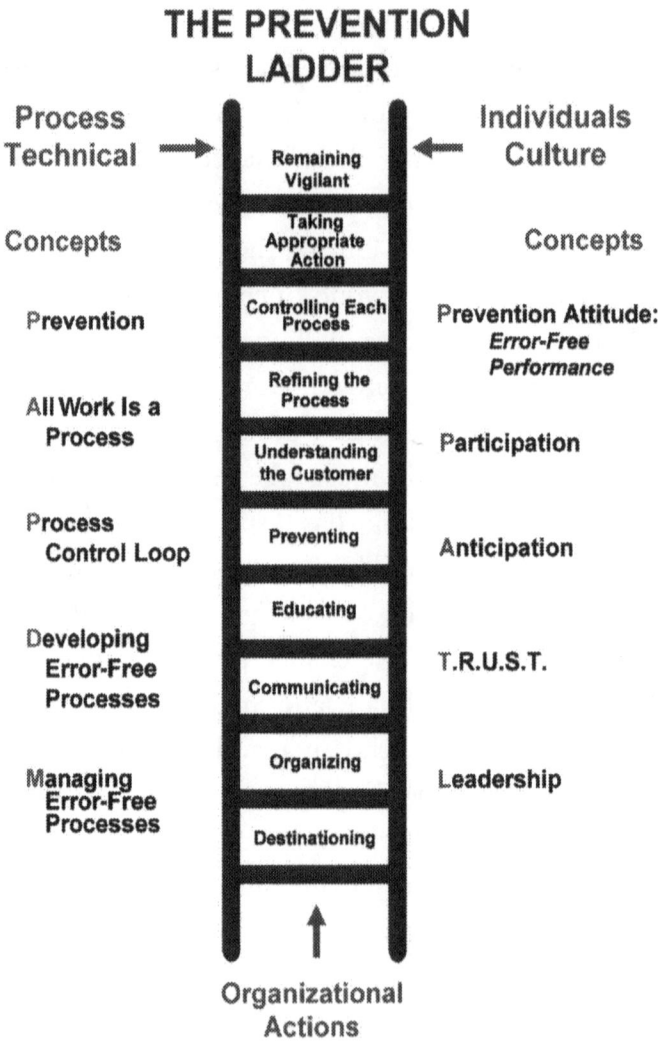

THE PREVENTION LADDER

Process Technical		Individuals Culture
	Remaining Vigilant	
Concepts	Taking Appropriate Action	Concepts
Prevention	Controlling Each Process	Prevention Attitude: *Error-Free Performance*
All Work Is a Process	Refining the Process	
	Understanding the Customer	Participation
Process Control Loop	Preventing	Anticipation
	Educating	
Developing Error-Free Processes	Communicating	T.R.U.S.T.
	Organizing	
Managing Error-Free Processes	Destinationing	Leadership

Organizational Actions

The Left Rail: Process Knowledge Base

The left rail deals with the knowledge required to design, operate, maintain, and manage preventive work processes. Parts of the knowledge represented in the left rail are well understood in some organizations. The part that is generally less understood is the knowledge required to create preventive processes that are error-resistant, if not error free.

Some of the information that is contained in the process knowledge base is:

- All work processes are conceptually the same, and the prevention of error is therefore applicable to any work process.

- The mechanisms that prevent MEDs can be defined and understood by everyone.

- Processes can be designed to minimize MEDs.

- Process control is an effective way to implement prevention.

- Management systems are necessary to assure the implementation and management of preventive processes.

The Right Rail: People Knowledge Base

The right rail represents the concepts, tools, and techniques for creating a preventive organizational culture. A preventive culture is one in which each and every associate enthusiastically participates in efforts that prevent MEDs. They are never satisfied with simply fixing them. For most organizations this is a major change in focus. The habit of preventing is contrary to many organizational cultures, especially those that take great pride in firefighting and problem fixing. Worse is a culture that does not view each associate as a viable source of enthusiastic preventive implementation.

As a general rule, the tangible elements that help shape formal organizational culture are well understood. Unfortunately, the tangible elements of organizational culture usually do not reflect the informal culture of the organization, and it is the informal culture that has an immense impact on organizational performance!

There are five basic culture-shaping elements necessary to create a preventive organizational culture:

- All associates must understand and become committed to the concept of error-free performance. People in an organization who shun the idea of error-free performance breed a counter-culture that undermines the support of prevention. Accepting the attitude of error-free performance is a behavioral requirement that must be established.

- The second cultural objective is participation by everyone. It involves not just participation, but the *enthusiastic* participation of all associates.

- The third objective of a preventive culture is anticipation. Anticipation is the ability of associates to do more than to just react to their environment. They must have the skill and knowledge to help them anticipate improvement opportunities. As everyone gains these abilities, a transformation of the organization from one that reacts to process, market, and environmental circumstances to one that is usually ahead of changing events will occur.

- The fourth behavioral objective of a preventive culture is TRUST.

- The fifth objective of the culture rail is to continually demonstrate preventive leadership, which is what the Ladder is all about.

The Rungs

The two rails of the Prevention Ladder are joined together by ten rungs. The rungs, taken together, provide a change management plan. This change plan is defined by the specific groups of actions that comprise each rung. A complete set of rungs provides all of the ingredients for creating and maintaining measurable improvement in the organization as well as for setting the direction for integrating improvement into the routine work processes of the organization. This plan is critical to the idea of leading the organization to prevention. These actions, tailored to the organization, must be driven by the knowledge contained in both the process and cultural rails.

Management's Action Groups—The Lower Five Rungs

The executive management team must take leadership actions to implement Planned Preventive Performance. The lower five rungs are the sole responsibility of the management of the organization. These rungs contain critical actions that put the resources in place that will enable every individual to perform the tasks they will be required to carry out as the organization evolves. In essence, the management rungs remove roadblocks to individual improvement actions and better focus the efforts of each individual employee. They are:

- **Destinationing.** Pardon the use of this nonword. It is meant to describe the undertaking of continuous actions that determine a consistently understood direction for the organization. These actions are intended to keep the organization on the best day-to-day path to achieve its long- and short-term objectives in an ever-changing environment. It is a task that never ends.

- **Organizing.** A group within the organization must be identified, at least temporarily, to plan the installation of prevention activities within every part of the organization. It is the responsibility of this group to keep senior management involved and keep the improvement efforts moving during the early part of the journey to prevention. During this beginning phase, the demands of the day-to-day routine work often outweigh and therefore stifle the efforts to install the systems necessary to improve.

- **Educating.** Knowledge is power, and in this case the knowledge is contained in the power of the rails. It must be delivered to everyone in the organization. This is an ongoing effort, not a short course. Because education and training have half-lives, educating is an unending effort.

- **Communicating.** The communication I am talking about here includes everything from the hallway chats to formal organizational communications. It must be constant, planned, consistent, honest, and at least two-way. It is only through communication that opinions can be changed and trust built. Like the ongoing tasks above, communication goes on and on.

- **Preventing.** The fifth rung deals with senior management's responsibility to deploy prevention throughout the organization. These efforts include providing all associates with the resources they will need to help the organization make every process as preventive as possible. This too is nonstop.

Everyone's Action Groups—The Highest Five Rungs

The top five rungs are action groups that must be carried out by each and every individual in the organization. They apply to everyone. This means executives, managers, and every single associate. No one is exempted. Every person is able to influence process performance directly in the work processes that they personally perform. Everyone can also indirectly influence work processes through supplier-customer relationships with which their personal work process interacts. Please pardon my repetition, but I want to be certain there is no misunderstanding. These actions are to be applied personally by everyone to his or her individual work process. Each individual, including the chief executive officer and all of the top executives of the company, should be working to improve the processes in which he or she is involved. These improvement activities include:

- **Understanding the Customer.** This group of actions is intended to encourage and provide support for each person to better understand not only his or her customer's requirements but also to understand the use the customer makes of his or her work outputs. Understanding areas such as how the customer's market is changing or changes the customer is planning to make will better position every associate to be a better supplier. This applies not just to external customers but to internal customers as well.

- **Refining the Process.** Any process can be refined based on observations made of the customer's experience with someone's work output. It can also be refined based on the associate observing his or her own process as he or she performs it. Frequently, better ways to do things are found. The process manager can also watch other similar processes to see if there is anything to be learned. Many organizations use benchmarking as a tool in this area of improvement.

- **Controlling the Process.** Every associate must take care to control his or her work process using the ideas contained in the Process Control Loop (PCL).

- **Taking Appropriate Action.** Each associate has a role in taking positive, preventive, and permanent corrective action when error occurs in his or her work process in order to prevent MEDs.

- **Remaining Vigilant.** Each associate must continuously search for ways to improve while also making certain that previously taken corrective actions remain in force.

This brief discussion of the various parts of the Prevention Ladder would not be complete if we did not discuss the part you cannot see. There is another vital part of leading prevention that must have a place in this discussion, even though it does not have a place in the Ladder: "enablers." These are the omnipresent topics that crop up in almost every discussion of prevention. I will take just a moment to highlight a few enablers to give you an idea of what I am talking about.

Enablers

Though not components of our Ladder construct, these general enablers positively support performance-improvement activities. They play an enabling role by creating conditions that make improvement activity less difficult.

- **Technology** is a great example. Technology has a place on both rails, in process control, documentation, and so on, and in online training technology and general administrative information systems. The application of technology has demonstrated tremendous gains in performance improvement in virtually all kinds of work processes to which it has been applied. Yet the development and production of technology makes technology itself an ideal candidate for the same performance improvement and prevention management necessary in any other work process. It should be noted that the application of technology itself may or may not result in performance improvement of the application. In fact, technology can reduce performance if its application is not thoughtfully planned and executed. We include technology as a universal enabler to the overall goal of improvement.

- **Communication Systems.** Organizations that have developed and operate efficient communication systems to provide information and feedback on a timely basis enjoy a tremendous advantage when implementing prevention management; their communication systems link people with leaders and with one another and support everyone's role as an internal customer and supplier.

- **Learning Resources**. Many organizations enjoy physical facilities and specialized staff catering to education and training. While seen as an indirect expense, this enabler is perhaps the soundest investment any organization can make to deal with the relentless demands of change and the typical reluctance of people to understand and accept new and different conditions that affect their processes. Knowledge is useless if it cannot be delivered into the minds of those who need it.

- **Project Management Skills.** Getting things done in an organized manner requires project management. Personal skills and technology can help here, but it all boils down to how well the organization is able to plan and to follow its plan to make changes.

- **Knowledge Acquisition Skills.** Smart organizations are able to seek, find, and acquire new knowledge and then to use that knowledge effectively to adjust and improve performance. Organizations that rely solely on an initial knowledge base defined at the time the organization was founded, as well as those that have little or no way of learning will have difficulty in the long run.

All organizations try to improve, and take many paths to reach that objective. In this environment, the Prevention Ladder is helpful by providing executives with a complete road map of the actions that must be taken to lead their organization to achieve Planned Preventive Performance.

4

Preventive Process Concepts, Design, and Management

◆

Left Rail

Preventive processes are created by completely defining their requirements and then managing them using the Process Control Loop.

All Work Is a Process

For many years, some people excused themselves from process improvement with the argument that process thinking does not apply to them. They argued that they were not in manufacturing or a processing business. They argued that they never saw a real customer, that they never did the same thing twice, or that they were performing some kind of elite function such as surgery, painting a mural, or building a nuclear power plant. All these excuses were intended to pardon them from looking at their work processes. It is always discouraging when people identify with the belief that their work is so different from what others do that there is no way the concepts and techniques of process improvement could apply to them. In fact, the issue is that they do not realize that their work is a process and that it is conceptually identical to any other process.

They lack the knowledge represented by the left rail of the Prevention Ladder.

They fail to see that a process is a series of steps that produces an outcome intended to satisfy a customer. If they are unable to recognize their work process as just one step along a chain of events leading from one supplier and customer to another, they cannot possibly see the basic nature of the tasks they perform.

The thought that some individuals do not see performing work as a process is worrisome. In fact, it is more than worrisome. This lack of understanding, or the misapplication of the understanding, remains one of the single most significant deterrents to performance improvement of any kind, and condemns the organization to fighting fires forever.

The pursuit of prevention begins with the understanding that all work is a process. Thinking of processes as being made up of a series of steps, conditions, or actions, provides a basis for analyzing them. The resulting analysis provides a fertile field for finding and eliminating the mechanisms that cause MEDs. Improvement opportunities often come with little effort or expense. All you must do is recognize work as a process and then identify the processes' customers and suppliers. Next, talk to those customers and suppliers about what you do in your process and ask them how they use what you provide them. It's no more difficult than that. One of the foundational concepts, therefore, of making prevention happen is understanding that all work is a process. This provides us with a common perspective from which to study all prevention opportunities anywhere in any organization and situation.

The process nature of work allows us to describe and analyze any work activity. Prevention is applied in both the planning of how work is done and also in the operation and management of each work process. When you think about performing simple tasks like making reservations for dinner, renting an automobile, or boarding an airliner, you will begin to get a feel for the process nature of the work being performed to make those things happen. While you, the customer, may see any of these activities as a one-time event (*your* dinner reservation, *your* rented auto, *your* seat on the airplane), it typically takes several steps or actions on the part of the restaurant, rental-car agency, or airline to take, document, and fulfill the reservation. Whatever it takes to meet your needs on this single occasion must be repeated over and over again for other customers. If the business is to be successful, there are many customers to be consistently served error-free reservations, just as you hopefully were. This is the simple logic of work processes. It is the basic language of improvement.

Processes generally have many steps that take place in a sequence to complete a job. When necessary, we can regard each of these steps as a mini process nested within a higher order, top-level work process. To understand most processes, we have to break them down into the individual steps it takes to complete a task. Take the surgical procedure of removing an infected appendix, for example. Many people are involved, many knowledge and skill sets are required, many steps are taken, and many eventualities have to be planned for in advance in order to assure success.

In order to achieve prevention, it is vital that each step of a process be well defined. It is also vital that what is to be performed in each step is clearly identified. Additionally, it is critical that how each step is to be performed is made clear. We call this process of defining and identifying, making clear the requirements for that step. Requirements are characteristics of the process and process output that are needed, desired, or mandated by the customers of the process. Requirements can be found in many places including contracts, work instructions, procedure manuals, and spec sheets. Requirements of a task include the inputs that will be utilized within the process to produce the desired outcome, the time when the job is to be complete, and the tools and techniques that will be used. There are other elements of the process that also must be defined.

If we use the appendectomy example, the requirements would provide the answer to some basic questions. For instance, it would be good to know what surgical instruments are needed when an appendectomy is performed. It would also be helpful to know the skill levels the nurses and doctors must have in order to perform the operation. And, oh yes, it would be helpful for the surgeon to be able to verify the identity of the patient and be assured that it is this patient who requires the appendectomy. Requirements are not only helpful but critical to prevention.

All too frequently, requirements are poorly defined, missing entirely, or obsolete. Such shortcomings cause problems ranging from improper staffing and improper planning to using outdated or erroneous inputs to the process. The results of having poor requirements are MEDs. The idea that all work is a process and that each step in each process is defined by requirements provides a basis upon which to build additional concepts of prevention.

The Process Control Loop

Building on the principle that all work is a process, we now can add another vital principle: all processes must be properly controlled. The Process Control Loop (PCL) is the tool we use to establish and maintain control of work processes and to achieve prevention during process operation. The elements of the Process Control Loop are shown. Please note how they are arranged in a "closed loop" configuration.

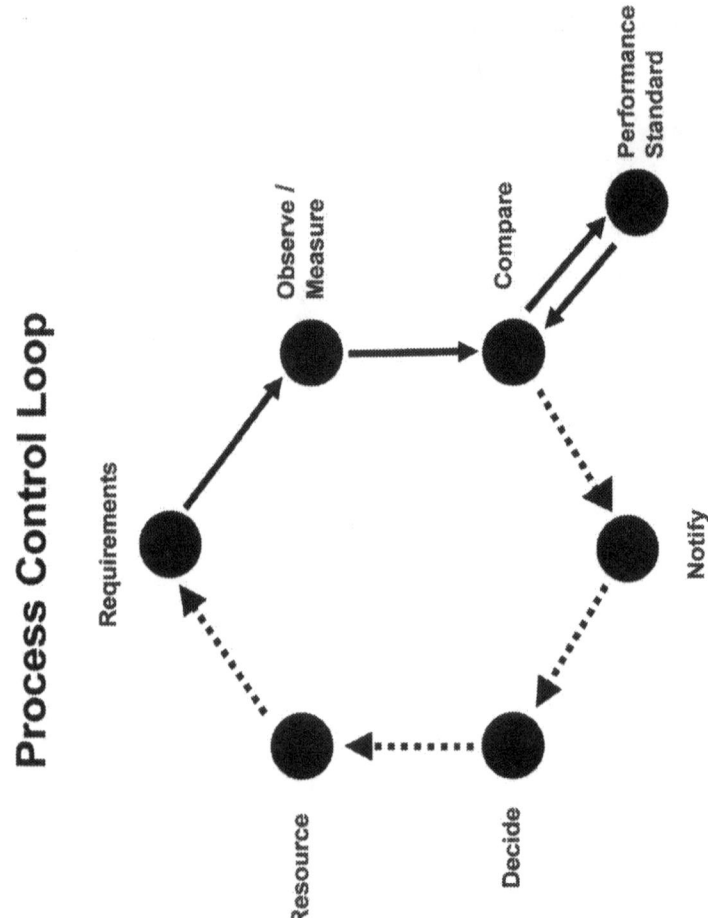

Process Control Loop

A scheme for proper process control must contain each and all of the elements shown in the loop, and the loop must be closed. The six required elements of a proper and complete process control system are:

- An identified process with well-defined **requirements.**

- A plan or method to **observe or measure** each iteration of the process.

- A method of **comparing** the observed iteration of the process or process outcome to a properly identified **standard of performance**.

- A technique by which the resource responsible for taking action to control the process can be **notified**.

- The resource responsible for taking action must **decide** if further action is to be taken.

- When notified, the **corrective resource** begins to take appropriate action both to return the process to a state of meeting the selected standard of performance and to prevent the situation from occurring in the future.

The purpose of process control is to make certain that each iteration of a work process follows all the requirements for that process. If the requirements are correctly defined, process control should assure that the process produces the desired outcome.

By way of review, we have discussed that the pursuit of prevention requires everyone to understand the first two basic concepts that create preventive processes. These two concepts are:

- All work is a process.
- The Process Control Loop is a graphic representation of the actions that must be taken to control a process.

Understanding these basic ideas gives everyone the foundation to understand the next two objectives in moving the organization farther along the journey to true prevention:

- Developing error-free work processes
- Managing work processes for error-free performance

Developing Error-Free Processes

Built on the basic concepts of prevention, developing and managing processes are the key activities in deploying preventive processes. There are proven ways that organizations can make prevention real in everything they do. The first of these is to design processes that minimize the chance that MEDs will occur.

Most processes are designed with the single-minded thought of getting the job done, to which is often added the undesirable dimension of "...at all costs." Once a process is designed or laid out, the formal requirements usually stay that way for years. As new methods are developed or as problems are found, the old way of doing things is just patched and crutched to keep things going. Seldom is the process reviewed to see if there are items that are inherent in the way the process is constructed or operated that make it prone to producing MEDs.

As an example, there are process designs that make some process flows more likely to have problems than others. Process flows that mix different types of operations at a single workstation requiring the frequent change from one tool or task to another create an increased opportunity for mistakes to occur. In some instances, the likelihood of mistakes might be reduced if the process were to be redefined so that it would be done in dedicated stations or with dedicated tools and equipment. In the office, there are document flows that cause an office employee to do several things that could be done better if organized in a different sequence. For instance, moving back and forth between computer screens can cause a loss of time and attention and can also contribute to mistakes.

There are some widely recognized rules of process design that offer some guidance to help reduce the chance of mistakes. An understanding of the mechanisms that cause MEDs is helpful in the development of processes that will have a minimal chance of creating problems for the organization. These rules should be employed frequently but are actually infrequently used. A simple example is the idea that any task should be mistake proofed if possible. It is a fact that few process developers know the ways to minimize the probability that MEDs will be created within the work process they are developing, much less how to mistake proof processes.

With proper understanding and forethought, we can define processes that are capable of operating without MEDs. When we accomplish this, we are halfway to our goal of total deployment of preventive processes.

Managing Error-Free Processes

While processes can be designed to minimize the opportunity for MEDs to occur, processes still must be managed in a manner that assures they will be operated as defined. Failure to pay attention to the minute-to-minute operation of the process is what brings surprises and problems. Processes that have not had the advantage of being designed with error-free performance in mind are more susceptible to being the source of trouble. Because they have not been cleansed of MED-causing mechanisms mentioned earlier, they are rife with opportunity for incident. Their performance is usually inconsistent and requires unusual amounts of patching, rework, and help.

The model for managing either poorly or preventively designed processes is the same. The Process Control Loop (PCL) is an extremely helpful visual that illustrates how processes should be managed.

Processes can be made to be preventive if management insists that the basic concepts of process prevention are fully utilized. There must be a single-minded focus on making process prevention a reality. Processes have to be developed in a manner that minimizes the chance of MEDs occurring and then these processes must be properly managed in order to benefit from the concepts of prevention.

5

Creating Preventive Cultures

✦

Right Rail

Technical tools cannot overcome weak management. Neither can enthusiastic management overcome the lack of properly utilized technical tools. Only together can they provide a strong, useful chain that leads to robust process performance.

In order to realize the benefits of Planned Prevention Performance, an organization must provide two things:

1. Direction as to what is to be done and the tools or systems to do the job

2. An environment that creates a desire within each and every associate to enthusiastically work to achieve the goals and objectives of the organization

Creating such an environment means that the management of the organization must develop a culture that nurtures the understanding and use of the concepts of prevention. Management has the responsibility, by virtue of its title and position, to lead the culture-shaping process. In order to build the foundation of a preventive culture, management must provide clear, constant, and consistent direction that supports, encourages, nurtures, and demands behavior that prevents MEDs. This behavior should be based on the knowledge from both rails of the Ladder. The knowledge of the left rail deals with how to make and to manage preventive processes. This knowledge base provides the "what to do." The right rail represents the knowledge base on how to get everyone to "want to" perform the processes as defined and "want to" lend their brains to the organization to help find ways to prevent MEDs.

The problem of how to mobilize the human resources of an organization to eagerly implement the technical systems and tools contained in the left rail is the domain of the right rail, the culture rail. Such a mobilization of human resources to practice prevention management requires that process workers have access not only to the tools themselves but also that they are engulfed in an organizational culture that creates and reinforces a true desire to use these tools all the time.

Even highly motivated, well-meaning individuals provided with the correct technical tools cannot cause processes to perform well in the absence of a preventive environment, an environment that encourages each associate to routinely and continuously take actions to prevent MEDs.

There are five concepts that are important in developing a culture that is error free:

- Attitude of error-free performance
- Participation
- Anticipation
- Trust
- Leadership

Each of these five is an intangible ingredient that creates and identifies a preventive culture.

Error-Free Performance

The concept of error-free performance is a performance standard. In this discussion, I am referring to the performance standards mentioned in Chapter Four during the discussion of the Process Control Loop. Performance standards are important because they tell us whether performance is good enough or not. If they tell us performance is not good enough, actions must be taken to make things better. By selecting the appropriate performance standard, we can establish a desirable level of performance. The performance standard will then alert us to take the necessary actions to improve the process.

Performance standards fall into two categories. The first category is a standard of "that's close enough" (TCE). When an observation of process performance is compared to this standard, the observed result does not have to meet the standard. It just has to be close to the standard. How close is always a subject for discussion. This standard means that the process does not have to be performed as planned (as defined by the requirements). It just has to be close to the requirements most of the time. TCE standards take the form of some acceptable number of MEDs (failures to meet the requirements) per a group of repeated measured process iterations. Examples of such standards might include three blank data fields in every ten loan applications submitted, 3 percent hang-ups before the phone is answered, and rental auto windows that must be free of streaks and smudges most of the time. Such standards insure that process requirements are not met all the time and that some customers will be disappointed sometimes.

The second category of standards requires that everyone strive to meet all the requirements all the time, every time. This performance standard is known as Zero Defects (ZD). The concept was created by Philip Crosby in the early 1960s. I prefer to use the term *error-free performance* rather than ZD. Improvement begins with a simple agreement that everyone will do his or her part to meet the requirements all of the time. When a situation arises in which there is a failure to perform as planned, the attitude of error-free performance directs efforts to prevent the situation from recurring. If the requirements are found to be incorrect, then everyone's commitment is to officially change the requirement to what is really needed.

In such an environment, management must lead by example. They too must commit and behave in a way that demonstrates the attitude of error-free performance.

Management intellectually understands that achievement of performance-improvement goals is vital to the long-term survival and success of the organization. As a result, they say and write the right words. Unfortunately, and all too frequently in the heat of the day-to-day, they condone short-term, nonpreventive actions. When such events occur, these occurrences are taken by the associates as examples of management's lack of commitment to the objective of preventive performance. Such events demonstrate to the associates that management is not dedicated to actually taking preventive actions all the time. As a result, the associates tend to follow these short-term examples by management in the operation of their own processes. These instances, in which management takes a shortcut to achieve a short-term goal, are not good. They are not good because they are counter to the long-term objective of doing things right and causing permanent improvement. They are worse because they show a management-behavior pattern that instigates and reinforces a cultural norm of "consider cost and schedule first and let prevention sort itself out later." Therefore, while the right leg of the Prevention Ladder deals with individual behavior and organizational culture, it really boils down to how personal attitudes shape the organization's culture. Prevention must be developed and nurtured by the way management exhibits preventive leadership.

Without the standard of error-free performance, everyone will understand that the things that go wrong do not have to be prevented. This concept is the glue that holds together all the efforts to make prevention real.

Participation

Participation means participation by everyone. In order to participate, to enthusiastically participate, associates must feel that their participation is wanted and appreciated. They must also feel comfortable in their participation. Some are reluctant to offer an idea because of shyness, fear of speaking up, or insecurity about how their ideas will be received. Management must build the confidence and ability of every associate so that each one is comfortable with and capable of participating. Management must also build a culture that not only encourages participation but also welcomes and rewards it by taking actions that provide incentives to those who participate. By incentives, I am talking about money and recognition, and I am talking about providing appreciation when an associate helps or tries to help. We want to build a culture in which everyone contributes his or her thoughts and efforts to cause prevention to become a reality.

Anticipation

Anticipation is the act of being ready to respond in an advantageous way to things that are about to happen. Without anticipation, every event must be dealt with or reacted to in an unplanned manner by whatever approach is available at that time. Without the preparedness caused by anticipation, responses to situations are largely left to chance.

You will recall the young Luke Skywalker in *Star Wars*. While in training to be a Jedi Knight, Luke learns from Master Yoda that the Jedi cannot tell the future but that they can read the present and anticipate it. They are so good at it that they might leave the audience with the impression that they can really see what is going to happen. In the great fun of movie fiction, Yoda is describing what we mean by anticipation.

Anticipation begins with the observation of what is going on around us and then the proper interpretation of these observations in the context of prevention. The information gained from observing and paying attention provides the foundation for anticipation. The next step is interpreting the observed occurrences. Interpreting some of these observations may not be simple without some basic tools. An example of a simple tool is a log of what happened, and when. This log allows us to see a series of events. With this information it can be possible to find a pattern that allows us to anticipate. On occasion the interpretation of these events may require some simple mathematical or statistical analysis to help identify the pattern and interpret the recorded observations. All of this activity can provide a basis for prethinking and preplanning. Thinking through a process or preplanning for future events depends on knowledge.

The greater the knowledge of the subject, the greater the ability is to foresee and anticipate potential trouble.

Do not be confused. I am not suggesting that anticipation provides a license to meddle in a process that is producing the desired outcomes. Moreover, neither am I advocating introducing an army that spends its time dreaming up what-if scenarios. Within the scope of preventive process control, anticipation is dependent on one's ability to observe and to interpret what is happening and to take action. This depends on knowing what to do, knowing how to monitor process performance, and then being ready to act to prevent process problems before they create MEDs. This is why anticipation is such a critical behavior in preventive cultures. Just as in everything else, it does not happen unless management provides the knowledge, support, encouragement, and resources to make it happen.

Acts of anticipation are made up of two opposite extremes of an action spectrum. Those on one extreme are actually reaction to a situation without benefit of prethinking or preplanning; those actions on the other extreme are actually prediction of a specific event (the purist form of anticipation: knowing what is going to happen and when it will happen). The best type of reaction comes as a result of research, training, study, focus, and practiced action. Prediction can be the result of analysis of observations made of real-world occurrences aided by the appropriate scientific tools. Exercises and efforts to improve reactive anticipation include practice, what-if planning, disaster plans, contingency plans, succession plans, and emergency drills. Efforts to achieve predictive anticipation usually involve strategy development, statistical analysis, and the study of process and individual behaviors. Even though predictive anticipation is more desirable, in many cases reactive anticipatory efforts provide the larger percentage of anticipation actions.

Anticipation goes well beyond application in just the basic work processes. Obviously, anticipation extends into the high-level strategic processes as well. At this strategic level, management can plan to create an agile organization and a business plan capable of responding to events as they occur.

Trust

Trust in relationships between individuals involves predictable behaviors. A history of predictable, consistent, positive behavior tends to lead to trust. If an individual can rely on what he or she thinks another individual will do in a given situation, then it can be said that they "trust" each other. A history of reliable behavior improves as the number of iterations of reliable behavior increases. Members of an organization who have trust do not have to spend excessive time checking to see that others do the things they promise. Trust also improves the mood of the workplace and improves the sharing of information. All these benefits of trust are necessary in a preventive culture.

The very nature of improvement involves change. Many have cited a basic human resistance to change. Individuals typically seek the comfort of routine, consistency, and regularity. Change usually has to be sold to the organization. A significant element of causing improvement, therefore, involves not just making people comfortable with change but also causing them to enthusiastically enlist in helping to facilitate change—trusting the outcome.

We need a better understanding, therefore, of how trust develops so that we can better use it to be preventive. When two individuals initially meet, each has an opinion of the other based on his or her biases and experiences. The only way that this initial impression can be changed is through communication. By communication, I mean all types, both verbal and nonverbal. As the communication process continues over time, either the trust will increase or decrease based on what is communicated and how the individuals view this communication. Trust that occurs in a relationship develops because of the cumulative effect of communications occurring between or among individuals. (Stay with me. This is not intended to make trite a subject that is often read as psychobabble and techno mumbo-jumbo.) Interpersonal communications can create relationships from which trust develops. It is no more difficult than this, but how it happens is somewhat complex. People have been dealing with communication as a problem since Adam met Eve, and maybe even before, when it was just between God and Adam. Nevertheless, it is critical in changing an organizational culture. This is not the place to provide details explaining relationship development, interpersonal communication, and trust. For now, understand that when we spell trust as T.R.U.S.T., it stands for the following key elements of communication between individuals:

- **T**ransaction (content of the communication *and* the style with which the message is communicated)

- **R**elevance (perceived importance of the message to the situation at hand)

- **U**niverse (environment within which the communication is taking place)

- **S**elf-Monitoring (the process of personally monitoring and adjusting the communication experience itself)

- Time (the effect of elapsed time over the eventual effect communication has on personal relationships)

With an understanding of these five components of communication (and ultimately of TRUST creation), communications can be prethought, preplanned, and carefully delivered to provide the best chance to build TRUST in the organization.

Leadership

Obviously, leadership is a critical part of changing an organization into one that habitually prevents. For that reason, we frequently refer to the Prevention Ladder as the Prevention Leadership Ladder. It provides a road map for leading an organization to prevention. Leadership, like prevention, appears to be well understood, but like prevention, it is easier to understand it intellectually than to make it happen. Leadership is simply taking actions that cause people to follow. Therein lies part of the problem. Leaders must answer: "What actions? What person or group of people? In what situation? To what destination?" There are many variables in leadership depending upon the answers to these questions. For example, leadership does not always happen with positive methods, for positive motives. When we say leadership, we usually mean using primarily positive methods and techniques to lead a generally willing group, toward a worthy end. That is not always the case, but for the purposes of this discussion, that is exactly what we are talking about.

We all know that leadership is situational. The particular techniques used in an instance are shaped by the situation at hand. Some leaders have only one style of leadership—a style that fits only certain specific situations. Some can do a great job of leading a start-up company but cannot lead one in a mature phase of its development. Others are great at turnarounds but lousy at leading an ongoing successful business. The leader's style(s) must be matched to the situation.

Leadership is dependent upon a couple of factors other than the situation. The followers must at least think that the leader knows where he or she is going and how to get there. As soon as they believe the leader is lost or does not have a correct path for getting to the destination, their willingness to follow diminishes. The followers must also think there is something in it for them when they reach the destination. They must feel they will gain something when the journey is over. The willingness of the followers to follow increases if the followers believe this leader is the only one who knows where to and how to lead them to their reward. If there are multiple leaders who can obtain for them their desired benefit, their loyalty to one leader is lessened. With these few observations about leadership behind us, I would offer these simple steps to leading:

1. Carefully assess and determine the situation.

2. Determine and define appropriate actions.

3. Select, prepare, and manage associates.

4. Take leading actions.

5. Use the Process Control Loop to manage the journey's progress.

The culture of the organization is the part of prevention that convinces the associates to play. If the culture is one that creates apathy, anxiety, or fear, it limits associates' willingness to participate. It reduces the attention they need to anticipate. Only in a trusting culture can management expect their associates to enthusiastically take part.

If the culture is one in which "that's close enough" is the performance standard for doing things, the usefulness of the best plans, processes, strategies, and intentions are of little minimal value. If, by example, the organization has taught the associates it's OK not to follow the plans and requirements all the time, things will not happen as desired. If the culture is wrong, the best plans and efforts created with help from the Ladder are of little value.

Now let's discuss one of the important characteristics of a preventive culture: following the requirements all the time, every time.

Snail Crossing

In the early 1980s, Philip Crosby Associates started teaching the Quality College in Europe. Our first client in Europe was IBM. During a session on Zero Defects, I was explaining the meaning of ZD. As examples, I cited the usual situations in which people expected no errors: accurate accounting on your paycheck, correct change from a cash transaction, air travel landings equal to takeoffs, and so on. An executive raised his hand.

"Do you mean that we should stop at all stop signs?" he asked.

"Certainly. Can you imagine how exciting it would be to drive if some people ignored some stop signs some of the time? The stop sign puts an order into proceeding through an intersection. Obeying it is a thing we all must do. When we all make a commitment to stop all the time and then live up to that commitment, that is the attitude of ZD," I lectured.

"What if I could see all roads approaching the stop sign and no one was coming?" he proposed. "Must I stop then?"

"Yes!" I replied. "If you break the habit of stopping at every stop sign, you might get sloppy and miss one when there's traffic approaching. And you must remember that we all overlook things on occasion. You may have overlooked a car. It's the right thing to do."

"What if I were in the middle of a desert and there was no cross-road, just a stop sign in the middle of a stretch of road that was seldom traveled?" he hypothesized.

"A good question. Can I ask you why you would not want to stop at this stop sign in the middle of a lonely desert road?" I responded.

"Because I can see there are no automobiles for miles, and there would be no need to stop at the stop sign," he countered.

"Why do you think the stop sign is for avoiding automobiles?" I challenged.

There was a moment of quiet without any answer.

I continued, "What if the stop sign was to protect a rare slow-moving snail that crosses the desert. And assume this snail provided food for a bird that scattered seeds from an exotic tree that provided nests for squirrels that ate nuts and left the broken shells that fertilized the ground that produced a flower that fed a very special butterfly that pollinated wine blossoms that made for a bountiful wine harvest? If you ran over one of these snails, it could be a mother or father of a whole bunch of snails. Without the snails...no wine," I proclaimed.

I continued, "Just because you do not know why a decision was made to place a stop sign at this point in the desert does not give you the right to run it. You may not have all the knowledge."

As I paused, there was no comment. I continued again. "Getting back to work at IBM, procedures, rules, methods, and standards are put in place for a reason. The reasons for many of them may not be obvious. But that is no reason not to follow those directions without exception. If you think the direction is a waste of time or has no purpose, ask someone who knows. If you determine there is no reason for the rule, then change it formally. Do not just ignore it. That is the meaning of ZD."

Later I knew that I had answered his question when the students began to talk to one another in the class workshops; I could hear them referring to the snail-crossing story.

6

Providing Preventive Leadership

◆

The Lower Five Rungs

Management must change its perspective on the organization. Traditionally, managers look up and down the organization. In a preventive organization they must learn to look horizontally and follow the processes until they reach the final customer.

The role of management in leading a preventive organization is very similar to the task of bringing a new product or service to market. Management must be sure that the organization knows what it is trying to accomplish, has a plan to accomplish it, and knows how to make it happen. Members of the organization must communicate with one another, have the resources to get the job done, and have some way to stay on course until the task is complete.

Rolling out a culture change and installing preventive tools and techniques in all work processes should be treated like any other major change. The lower five rungs of the ladder represent five groups of actions that must be taken by management to provide the leadership foundation and plan that will allow all associates to do their part (the highest five rungs) in transforming the organization into one that routinely achieves Planned Preventive Performance.

Destinationing

The Destinationing rung involves deciding where the organization is going and how it is going to get there. A destination must be kept current as technology, the market, the economy, and other factors change. It is like getting on an airliner in Atlanta for a trip to Seattle: The CEO of the airplane, the pilot, has to know where he or she is headed with absolute specificity. He or she further has to have a flight plan for how the airplane will proceed. The pilot will be aware of environmental variables such as headwind, temperature, and air traffic, and from this information, he or she will estimate the flight time and the arrival time. This plan is based on the best information available at the time. The flight crew usually advises the passengers of the route and estimated arrival time and provides any other information they feel the passenger might need to know to make them feel comfortable. As the flight progresses, things can and often do change. If the change is significant, like weather in the flight path or stronger headwinds than anticipated, the plan may be changed. If a major change to the flight plan is made, the pilot will probably inform the passengers.

In this example, the pilot and the supporting cast of ground crew, air-traffic controller, and airline management are "Destinationing." Their actions require that the aircraft be prepared for the trip, the flight plan filed, the checklist reviewed, the passengers loaded, the safety talk given, and on and on. In flight, the crew pays attention to the developments along the flight path and makes changes to the plans as events unfold. Informing the passengers makes most passengers feel more comfortable, safer, and somewhat more in control of their destiny. Destinationing involves prethinking, planning, communicating, and, when necessary, inventing on the run.

Ask any chief executive if he or she has a current strategic plan, and you will be assured that his or her organization has a plan that spells out the organization's direction in some detail. You will also hear that the plan is current and adequate to provide the planning of the organization's future. That plan probably was developed using a common pattern consisting of analyses of strengths, weaknesses, opportunities, and threats; strategy: tactical plans; list of goals and objectives (usually accompanied by at least high-level measures); and detailed action plans. There is a good chance that the CEO will volunteer that the action plans are revisited on a regular basis. All of this is good, and all are parts of the Destinationing group of actions.

But if you go into the organization and ask an associate about his or her understanding of this plan and how the associate's personal actions contribute to achieving that result, you frequently find that he or she does not have the information needed to fully and enthusiastically participate. The pilot is not keeping the passengers informed so that they may feel comfortable, safer, and somewhat in control of their destiny.

There are many facets of Destinationing. For example, Destinationing should include a constant effort to pay attention to the sociological, political, economic, technological, regulatory, and geographical changes that occur virtually every second of every day. These changes constantly stir the pot and must be accounted for. A management team can miss opportunities to alter its flight plan. It can drive its organizations into a solid wall of realities that threaten the organization's survival simply because it did not notice some small change in the environment soon enough, or because they failed to detect a trend developing right under their noses. In other words, Destinationing is asking management to use prevention techniques to reduce the chance of mistakes and errors while steering the organization to the desired destination.

Another component of the Destinationing rung is the accumulation of the knowledge the organization currently possesses that deals with prevention. It could involve lessons learned for designing and managing error-free work processes. The range of topics is broad and includes anything that would be useful in creating a preventive culture. This knowledge provides the specific codified experience that can populate the two rails of the Ladder. Without the knowledge that makes up these two rails, the Ladder is not much of a ladder. At least I would not want to climb it.

An organization should, therefore, have a priority to capture and codify both its implicit and explicit knowledge of how to make things better. Such a knowledge base can be leveraged to help eliminate MEDs in the specific organizational setting.

These are some examples of what makes up Destinationing. It involves more than strategy, but strategy is part of it. Destinationing is a process, like all work, that continuously observes the environment, interprets what it sees, and then takes the necessary steps to anticipate.

Destinationing is a process that consists of several actions. Among them are:

- Continuous observation and analysis of all elements of the environment
- A valid theory of the business

- A viable business model

- Vision

- Mission statements

- Targeted results

- Budgeting

- Product planning

Destinationing is the first of the five organizational groups of actions that rely on management for their planning and execution. What is the old saying? "If you don't know where you are going, any road will get you there." Destinationing is knowing where you are going and which road to take to arrive there.

Organizing

Planning for the implementation of the actions of the ten rungs does not happen by itself. It is obviously important, but in the beginning some will see it as extra work. It is work, however, that must be done. Sometimes in the heat of the day-to-day struggle, the emphasis on improvement is lost, and business as usual takes over. Planning and follow-up is superseded by the regular fighting of fires. It is advisable, therefore, to set up an ad hoc group from management that is responsible to plan the activities represented by the rungs of the Prevention Ladder. There are several guidelines that are helpful in setting up this planning and coordinating group:

- Assignment to this planning group is not a full-time job. Part of the way preventive management breeds prevention managers is by sharing the experiences of planning the organizational actions that make up the rungs. As with any process,

the members of the planning group can be changed as
needed, but it is recommended that a core group of members
remain unchanged to provide continuity.

- As previously mentioned, this is an ad hoc group. It will
  meet only until the implementation process is well-
  grounded and has become a part of the routine management of the organization.

- The group should have a broad representation from all the
  functions of the organization. (In an organization with multiple work sites, recognize that much of this effort is site specific.) Well-planned and well-managed status meetings
  (communications) with this planning group must be a priority and should occur at least weekly in the beginning.

- The top-level planning group frequently assigns a member to
  oversee the planning and monitoring of one of the other ten
  action groups. "Rung Champions" can select others from
  within the organization to assist in the specific planning and
  follow-up of their assigned rung's actions.

Educating

Organizations that have the facilities and/or staff-training profes-
sionals already on board have a clear advantage. These people act as
enablers especially in fulfilling the responsibility of improving
employee knowledge and skills. Any process change that finds its
way through to implementation requires some degree of employee
education and training in order to successfully implement the
change. Additionally, there is training necessary to disseminate the
basic knowledge contained in the two knowledge bases described as
the left and right rails. Without this requisite knowledge, associates

do not have the capability to help improve processes and relationships. Some important and maybe obvious points regarding education and training to be considered are:

- Education and training each have a half-life. Their benefit seldom lasts forever.

- Educating includes both value education and skill training.

- Education should help the associates understand the organization's processes, procedures, and products/services.

- Improving the value of associates can frequently best be achieved by providing each with better general knowledge and training. Such education and training may be aimed at providing the associate with confidence, team skills, communication capability, language, and improved technical knowledge.

- There should be the usual plan for which associates are going to be educated, in what area they will be trained, and when the instruction should occur. The plan must provide for ongoing training, from new-hire orientation to routine-skills-upgrade training, and training in the basic tools and techniques that help deploy prevention.

Communicating

Communication is the lifeblood of a smoothly functioning organization. It keeps everyone informed and provides the feedback that is necessary to manage any process. Few areas in business are as fragile as communication, which can easily be handled incorrectly. Thoughtful planning is needed to eliminate MEDs from the communication process. Structuring communication helps to keep the focus and attention on the importance of prevention. A preventive organization must devise a plan to assure adequate formal and informal communication about improvement efforts.

As previously pointed out, communicating includes all forms of dialogue: verbal and nonverbal, formal and informal, at work and off-site. It includes meetings and hallway discussions, e-mail, newsletters, and blogs. No avenue should be ignored.

Communicating also includes the formal rewards and recognition systems that help to demonstrate what it takes to be a hero in the culture. These recognition systems involve both monetary and nonmonetary rewards. They include raises, bonuses, promotions, and other employee-recognition processes and team rewards. The current status of improvement, corrective actions, and results are also important facts to communicate.

Associates must be told what is happening in order to minimize their dependence on grapevines and rumor mills. If management does not tell the associates what is occurring, the associates will make up stories of their own. I can assure you that you will like your stories better.

Preventing

The Preventing rung deals with the responsibility of management to deploy the knowledge, equipment, procedures, and systems that enable the organization to achieve Planned Preventive Performance. Prevention is dependent on the tangible support management gives the organization's employees by providing them with resources to design and operate work processes preventively. Especially critical processes must be identified and reviewed first with the intention of making each error free. As time and resources permit, the other processes should be reviewed, and the mechanisms that introduce the chance for MEDs must be identified and eliminated.

The search for improvements that can be made in processes never ends. After processes have been made resistant to MEDs, they must be managed using properly planned Process Control Loops and continuously reviewed for opportunities to improve their performance.

The management action groups of Destinationing, Organizing, Communicating, Educating, and Preventing provide management with the plan that enables the organization to move toward true prevention. These actions set the stage for the performance of the top five rungs. They will be performed by everyone but need the foundation provided by these bottom five rungs.

The following case provides a glimpse of an organization that needs to start thinking about prevention. This organization is too comfortable with the find-it-and-fix-it approach. It is providing resources but for the wrong reasons. I hope this case is not too familiar.

Lost Files

The executive meeting of a large insurance company had gone well. Many of the issues that had recently plagued the offices were discussed, and another round of actions had been identified. It had been a bad couple of months when it came to quickly finding the information needed to handle claims. The necessity of contacting the claimants, the employers, and the various medical entities to obtain information for the second time had delayed the payment of some claims. A few complaints a day should be expected, but this situation was snowballing and getting out of hand. Many clients were growing restless. Immediate action was necessary to remedy the situation.

It was determined that some temporary people would be engaged to help search for and replace the misplaced eligibility and claim information. It was estimated that if forty temps were hired, it should only take a couple of months or so to get things back on track. Some special teams had been formed, and action plans were to be defined and agreed upon.

As Jim, Janet, and Keith left the conference room, Jim remarked that it was a good thing that the organization was having such a good quarter and was ahead of plan. "Even after the extra expenses we just agreed on, we'll still be ahead of plan."

Keith responded, "You're right! Let's make it happen so we can get back to normal."

Janet chimed in, "It seems we just have to go through this every once in a while. I believe it's part of the business." Both Jim and Keith agreed.

The actions taken to remedy the situation progressed but not without some difficulties. The task force assigned to hire the temporary people and get them oriented went without a hitch. A second task force identified and engaged a temporary-staffing agency on a long-term basis so that the next time this happened, time would not be lost finding a temp agency. The task force had to agree to a retainer, but that was expected and seemed worth the expense to save a few days next time. The third task force's charter was to find and lease the equipment that the temporary people would need to do their jobs. After the equipment had been identified, this team would see that the equipment was set up and operating within the time frame identified.

This last group ran into a major glitch. The company was still running an older version of the operating system software. Additionally, the tasks to be performed by the temporary employees would have to be completed on the company's proprietary, legacy software. This company-developed software could not be sufficiently scaled up without some additional modifications. Unfortunately, the IT group had a full schedule and would have to bump another project to make time for the software upgrade. As a result of this situation, there would not be enough equipment available in the time frame necessary to meet the need.

When the situation was explained to the executive committee, the members of the committee decided that a limited number of pieces of equipment would be leased and that the task force would plan a work-around method that would not require computers. They would just do it the old-fashioned way: by shuffling paper. This work-around dictated that an additional twenty-five temps would have to be hired. It was lucky the company could afford it.

Many organizations spend their time and resources responding to problems as they occur. Efficiently dealing with mistakes, errors, and defects becomes a way of life—a culture. It seems there is never enough time or enough motivation to make prevention real. But there is always time to do it over.

7

A Preventive Organization in Action

✦

The Top Five Rungs

"Everyone" includes managers as well as associates. It is best to think of these five rungs applying to anyone and everyone in the organization.

After having examined the previous parts of the Prevention Ladder, we come to the last and maybe the most important part, the top five rungs. These top five rungs address the day-to-day application of prevention concepts and tools in every process used by every associate in the organization. Each individual must maximize his or her personal effort to permanently eliminate MEDs. The objective of the top five rungs of the ladder is to put systems in place that encourage, support, and reinforce each individual's prevention actions. Specifically, the organization as a whole must act to support individuals who:

- Have accepted the concept of error-free performance
- Are capable of participating and anticipating
- Know how to manage a process

- Know their roles in eliminating mistakes
- Are enthusiastic about the chance to help the organization realize Planned Prevention Performance

As we look at the top five rungs, or action groups, we recognize the words that have been used throughout the earlier chapters of this book. Words and phrases like *customer, process, process control, taking action,* and *vigilance* are old friends we have discussed before. The earlier chapters dealt with the knowledge bases of the theory and practice of error-free processes and cultures. Then we looked at the steps management must take to put the resources in place to enable each employee to achieve routine, habitual error-free performance. These last five rungs represent the actions everyone must take in order to take advantage of and apply this knowledge.

If things have gone as planned and if each associate is applying the ideas of how to implement prevention, the members of the organization will soon find no need to scramble to make up for things gone wrong or to cancel plans with their families because they are unexpectedly needed at work. These last few rungs are the payoff from the preparation and support provided in the work that has gone before. When that preparatory work has been properly performed, the achievement of error-free processes will pay big dividends.

Understanding the Customer

One of the greatest truths understood during the quality-management era is the recognition that everyone has customers, frequently many of them. The notion that the term "customer" applies only to the person at the end of the supply chain, who actually uses your organization's product or service, has given way to the broader recognition that your customer is also the person to whom you provide information, product, service, or attention. This includes the investment community, the management team, coworkers, people in other functions, even people whom you think serve you and your process! We normally call them suppliers, but in fact they are customers too, because we must deliver our requirements to them. We must also provide them with feedback about how their products or services are performing. It is surprising for many to learn that everyone within the organization is a member of a chain of customers and suppliers.

This being the case, it follows that the more we know about our customers, the better we can understand and anticipate their needs. This better understanding of our customer's current needs can lead to a better understanding of their future needs. Such knowledge makes it possible for us to plan so that we can be of value to them. We need to know more than simply what they expect from us today. It is helpful to know such things as how they use our outputs and any changes they plan to make within their process that could affect out work product. Such understanding can provide a chance for us—supplier and customer—to work together, and add increased value to the relationship.

The idea of simply complying with current requirements can lead to complacency. Some erroneously think that if the customer has not complained, things must be all right. Nothing causes a ruder awakening than to have a customer suddenly go elsewhere for something that we could have provided had we known what they wanted.

Many believe that marketing, sales, and the strategic-planning function should provide the ultimate awareness of what the customer needs. Little thought is given to the other customers who do not fall within the domain of marketing and sales. Seldom do we have the systems and methodology in place to encourage the average associate to develop better insights into their customers' needs. These customers may be at the next desk or at the end of a phone line.

Understanding customers requires that we practice frequent communication. This especially applies to internal customers. We have all seen departments that have a direct supplier-customer dependence on one another, where the individuals in each department have never taken the time to walk down the hall to see what the other departments do and how they do it.

Understanding the customer's needs is fundamental to preventing MEDs. You cannot leave prevention of MEDs to sales and marketing functions when much of their time is spent in appeasing dissatisfied customers. Understanding the customer means that we are not dependent on our customers to pass information our way. Preventive organizations do not exist in a state of waiting, hoping that the customers will tell them what they should know.

There are many techniques that provide us with customer insight. The simplest one is simply asking them questions. What do they want from us? How will they use our work products? How will their customers use our work products? From such an exchange, much of the basic information can be identified. Other techniques include observing customers in the act of using our product, listening to them talk about future plans, obtaining feedback on how our work product is performing in their environment, and conducting simple periodic reviews of the status of the relationship. Efforts to maintain a close relationship with customers requires a deliberate effort that must be not be left to chance.

This is why an entire rung of the ladder is devoted to customer understanding. It is key and, in many cases, is not being done. We must think of customers as the source of our success. After all, the more successful our customer is, the better we survive.

Refining the Process

Processes are defined by their requirements. Requirements tend to evolve over time. Sometimes these evolutions are not a good thing. Requirements that describe a process are not always as good as they should be. They may become unnecessary or obsolete. They may reflect a method of doing the job that can be improved. Where would you go to find a person who could tell you the most about improving a process's requirements? The person that usually has the best ideas on how to improve a process is the process operator or manager. After all, that is the person providing the hands-on management of the process.

The kind of information we are looking for generally comes from three basic sources. One type of information comes from observing iterations of the selected work process. In this environment, working the Process Control Loop enables us to monitor the processes performance. Frequently, the operator will notice better ways for the process to be done. This can cause a refinement to the requirements for how the process is performed. It can also result in a refinement in the final requirements of the process output.

A second typical source of information in which we are interested when we are refining the process comes from the user of our work output, or customer(s). Generally, the customer's information leads to refinements to the requirements in the final work output.

The third common source of process refinement is the suppliers of the inputs used in the process. Suppliers can sometimes see opportunities within the process that are not apparent to the process operator. Many times supplier inputs can provide refinement to the requirements related to what is to be done in the process and how it is to be done. Of course there are other sources that can provide information that leads to process refinement such as internal technical functions, regulatory agencies, agencies that produce standards such as the International Standards Organization (ISO), and use of the best practices, or benchmarking techniques.

Process operators/managers should always be alert for ways to improve process performance. Naturally, any changes being considered must be reviewed with the appropriate organizational functions and must be formally documented. The key activity of this rung is quite simply a constant, conscious effort to improve performance. This should be done with an eye toward anticipating the improvement. It is one thing to have an organization that can respond; it is entirely another to have an organization that anticipates.

Controlling the Process

This rung deals with the use of the Process Control Loop (PCL) by each associate as he or she operates his or her work processes. The PCL is what enables a process operator to actually manage his or her process, rather than be managed by it. In order to use the PCL, some decisions must be made. For example:

- What process(es) will I control?
- Do I know the requirements?
- How will I observe or measure the process performance?

- What is the performance standard I will use to determine if the process is performing correctly or not?

- If the process is not performing correctly, whom do I notify? (Frequently the operator, or process manager, is the one responsible for taking action to restore the process performance.)

- Who will make the decision on whether or not to take action?

- Who is responsible for taking the appropriate preventive action?

When every associate routinely uses the PCL to manage his or her work process, this associate will be controlling the process. This is an unending set of activities that go on with each iteration of the work process.

Taking Appropriate Corrective Action

The ninth rung ensures that the individuals of the organization have a planned, systematic way of dealing with situations in which processes do not perform as desired. Whether those problematic situations are discovered by routine use of the Process Control Loop or are found as a result of improved customer understanding, corrective changes must be made in an orderly manner. Without corrective changes, or corrective action, improvement cannot occur.

Remember: No Change = No Improvement.

Unfortunately, uncontrolled change can be detrimental to process performance and improvement. To prevent uncontrolled change requires that there be a documented, well-planned system. Corrective actions must be followed from the determination that something needs to be done to the successful follow-up of those actions taken. This follow-up must be taken to verify that the issue has actually been resolved.

As each associate is continuously monitoring his or her work processes and notifications are being made that improvement action is warranted, the worst thing that can happen is nothing. The next worst thing is that whatever happens occurs later than it should. And the final worst thing that can happen is that there is no follow-up that ensures the corrective action solved the potential for more unsatisfactory process outputs. At various times, each associate might have some role in this corrective process. That role might be assisting in the collection of data or information, verifying that the process output meets requirements, or participating in a corrective-action-definition meeting. Each of these roles is important to the idea of prevention. This rung provides the muscle for the concept of prevention.

Remaining Vigilant

I like the idea of vigilance. In this world of identity theft and the war on terrorism, vigilance should be our standard operating procedure. We all must be constantly watchful for threats to our well-being. That is exactly the idea of this last rung. As the organization moves toward the achievement of routine Planned Preventive Performance, it will require that each associate be vigilant to the mechanisms that cause MEDs. There are two activities that are necessary in order to remain vigilant in a preventive organization.

- The first is to be continuously looking for ways to improve. If we grow complacent or satisfied, entropy will take over. We must always search for ways to improve.

- The second is to keep corrective actions that eliminate MED-causing mechanisms in place. If a correction put in place to eliminate a MED is allowed to decay or be forgotten, the MED will come back and we will lose the gain that was made.

There are at least two enemies of vigilance. Routine and success each can cause inattention to work processes. Management must provide systems that minimize the impact of these two villains. We must continuously strengthen our efforts to be vigilant and to pay close attention to our work processes all of the time. Activities planned and carried out in the Communicating and Educating rungs need not search far for subject material. Reminders of the need for improvement and for keeping previously defined improvements in place are always ready topics.

If each associate within the organization habitually practices these five activities, prevention will be on the march. Results will begin to pile up and associates will have more time with their families. Oh yeah, you'll have more fun too!

Let's see the result when process managers do not routinely practice the highest five rungs. It probably happens more than you think.

Control Shack Case

In the early 1980s, I was assigned as an account executive for a petrochemical company. I think I got the assignment because I'm from Texas and it was, therefore, believed that I must know something about the oil business. In truth, I knew next to nothing about the business, but fortunately I did understand the concepts and techniques of improvement.

The first task of this new assignment was to become familiar with the client's production group. I was on an orientation tour of refineries in the United States, where the client was just beginning the improvement process. They still had a lot of doubts about whether this quality-improvement stuff could be applied to the refining business. They understood it applied to automobiles and televisions. But autos and TVs are items that can be counted. They reasoned that it was simple to recognize a defective TV or car, but they did not make units of distinct countable objects. They had constant streams of products that ran through pipes twenty-four hours a day, 365 and a quarter days a year. Most of the processes did not shut down except for overhaul or repair. It seemed to them that it would be hard to apply quality to the job of managing a process industry. They had particular difficulty applying the idea called Zero Defects to pipes of flowing fluids.

My guide through the facility was the maintenance manager. He was very helpful, but skeptical. He described how the processes were controlled. They had a very advanced Honeywell process-control system that was housed in what they called the control shack. The shack had several computer displays, each of which was monitoring different parts of the process. Each display showed a schematic of a part of the refining process. This screen displayed summary measurements and indicators on the top-level diagram of the process. This top-level summary screen was backed by other subscreens that provided additional detail to subprocesses within the top-level process. The technician could click on a part of the larger process to see more detailed information on the subprocesses. When a measurement was within control, or within tolerance, the screen was green. When the measurement exceeded the tolerance performance standard, the screen would turn red to alert the operator that some action needed to be taken. A sound accompanied the red screen to make certain that the out-of-tolerance condition was noticed. The job of the technician was to monitor the various subscreens by frequently switching to each screen to look for troublesome situations that had not set off an alarm.

This sounded very good. I asked to see the system in action. As we went into the shack, the manager selected one of the operators to show the system that he had described.

"This screen is the overview of the processes I monitor," he began. He provided other details of the process as he went through the process flow. He then switched to a second screen of a subprocess. The screen was green, and he explained that this screen showed that everything was operating nominally. Knowing I was a quality consultant, he produced a procedure manual and showed the description of the monitoring process he had just described. Again, I was impressed. Things were well controlled. I had nothing to add to the situation.

As we were about to leave, I asked one final question. "How many subscreens do you have to monitor?"

"There are twelve screens," he answered.

"Could I see them?" I asked.

He nodded and started slowly clicking through the screens. He had gone about halfway through the series of screens when he opened a screen that was red. I looked at the maintenance manager and asked, "Doesn't that mean there is a problem?"

The manager looked at the screen. I could see he was surprised. The technician began to explain. "This is not a problem. This process has a very tight tolerance. The tolerance is actually too tight. We can exceed the tolerance quite a bit and still be OK."

"Then why don't you change the tolerance to reflect the real values?" I inquired.

The manager interrupted, explaining that there were more important issues being dealt with than this relatively minor problem.

"Where is the audible alarm that accompanies the red screen?" I pursued.

"I turned it off so it wouldn't drive us crazy," the technician answered.

I asked the manager if there was a procedure that documented this work-around process. He said there was not.

I thanked the staff in the shack and we left the building. On our way to the office I summarized for the manager: "This is an example of the lack of the attitude of ZD. How many of these informal work-arounds do you have in the plant?"

"There are some," he admitted, "but they're just on things that aren't very important."

"But if you don't know how many there are, how do you know they're not important?" I quizzed. "Maybe the processes are not in control after all. Maybe there is waste created that is caused by this attitude that being close is OK sometimes. How do the employees know what rules are to be followed and which ones can be worked around?"

He had no answer for me.

If an organization is to create a truly preventive culture, it needs the help of everyone in the organization. All individuals must perform their jobs and verify that they are doing what has been planned. If things go awry, the organization needs the constant attention and the brainpower of these individuals to prevent these things from going awry again.

8

Getting Results

✦

Cashing the Prevention Check

The hardest part of getting started is getting started.

Most people can easily identify with the idea of prevention. People understand prevention when it deals with flights on airplanes, medical procedures, and payrolls. All too frequently, however, that is where the understanding ends. A surprising number of people have a difficult time believing that prevention is a viable approach for improvement in their organization, much less that it can be a major source of additional profit.

We know that customers rightly expect organizations to perform as they say they will. The natural motivation to do your very best is intrinsic to success in the marketplace, but doing your best should not include a mix of doing things wrong. Repeatedly making MEDs is a recipe that can eventually drive an organization to extinction or can at least make it difficult to struggle from one quarter to another, carrying the burden of wasted opportunities and wasted money.

More than thirty years of experience have taught me that if you stop doing things wrong, which requires extra effort to fix or replace things, you save money. It is hard to imagine that this is not the case. The money the typical organization can save is huge—30 percent of its operating costs. My experience has further shown me that about half of that amount can be recovered within two years. That amounts to 15 percent of operating costs saved per year, either forever or until the organization becomes complacent and stops paying attention to preventive actions. It seems to be worth pursuing this kind of result, but it takes commitment, dedication, attention to detail, and real leadership. As prevention begins to take hold, the tangible result realized from prevention-based processes sells itself. The resulting savings provide the best source of resources that may be needed for further improvement.

If you want to begin to get results and recover the money you are currently wasting, start by determining how much you are wasting because you choose to produce MEDs. After you get the number, determine where you are; by which I mean, how large will the task be to install prevention throughout the organization?

I suggest taking an inventory of what you have done previously that can be used as a foundation for adding any concepts, tool, techniques, or system that will be required to achieve Planned Preventive Performance. Think about the effort you put into quality management, statistical process control, reengineering, ISO 9000, applications for the Malcolm Baldridge Award, or Six Sigma. Add these to the normal approaches you have always had in place. These might include problem solving, project management, and your performance-measurement system. Determine how many of these still exist and are still used. If any part of these initiatives were successful and remain in use, they can be used as cultural anchors for adding organization-wide prevention.

Once you understand what you currently have in place, look at the Ladder and determine what is missing. Design an implementation plan to acquire the appropriate knowledge and install it in the organization. Set about measuring the results of installing prevention throughout the organization and quantifying the resulting benefits. Make the benefits real by following them to the bottom line. Consider the following results-recovery plan.

Five Steps for Tracking Improvements to the Bottom Line

1. Identify the components that cause waste. Estimate the cost to fix them or make up for the fact that they occurred. There are two basic types of costs:

   - Those that are caused by materials that are wasted or reduced in value because of the problem

   - Those incurred because people perform tasks that would not be necessary if the problem did not exist

2. Take the preventive actions necessary to eliminate the cause(s) of the loss of profit.

3. After the cause of the profit loss has been eliminated, the material component of the estimated waste will fall to the bottom line because materials will no longer be lost or degraded. Usually there is no additional effort required. The people costs that are eliminated by the preventive action(s) will *not*, however, automatically fall into the bottom line. Other actions are required if those savings are to be realized.

4. Identify the specific human resources affected by the improvement. Once the individuals are specifically identified, a determination must be made as to their future deployment. The nature of the disposition decision will determine where the benefit flows. If the disposition is to

terminate the individual(s), then the saving will show on the bottom line. Of course the savings will be net after any termination costs. If the individual(s) is to be reassigned to more productive jobs, then there will be no immediate bottom-line savings, but there will be an associated gain in productivity, as long as the performance targets for the acquiring function are adjusted to reflect the addition of new resource(s). If neither of these two deployments is done, as a minimum, the impacted human resource(s) should be isolated from the process that has been improved. Without management action, individuals left to continue in nonproductive jobs provide no positive result. Even worse, resources left in place without reassignment to productive responsibilities will speed the natural tendency of the improvement to atrophy. Frequently, this lack of management action produces acutely negative results and executive disillusionment with the improvement effort.

5. The quantified monetary results of the preventive action taken must continue to be tracked. The tracking of these results should encourage reinforcement of the corrective actions taken to prevent them from degradation. In the case of personnel reassignment, the performance of the organization that was the recipient of the saved resources should be monitored to assure that the planned benefit from the added resources is achieved.

If this simple procedure is used, the results of effective actions taken will show tangible results. Such measurable results will provide evidence that improvement is real. These results will spark other improvements and encourage the organization to continue to focus on prevention as a source of profit.

Getting Started

I would encourage you to begin today to dedicate your organization to prevention. The first step in getting started is to decide to get started. The sooner you decide, the quicker the benefits will accrue. I know there are reasons many may not start immediately. Over the past years, I have repeatedly encountered several obstacles articulated by executives in such a way as to make it seem as if their organizations were unsuited to the concepts and techniques being discussed. I sincerely believe that these objections were nothing more than a typical response of individuals unwilling to accept the idea that they had to change the way they did things. After all, they had a fair previous quarter. Or their plates were full. Or they could see the work that is involved in adopting a different way of managing. Let me try to get some of these objections out of the way now.

One-Third of Your Operating Cost Is Waste!

Wow, does that hurt! My experience has been that when executives first hear this, they do not believe it. It is not until some of their key associates are taken through an exercise to estimate the waste that the reality of this number sinks in. Again, my experience has been that this is a typical number. Yes, it varies a bit by industry, but overall I believe it was written on that stone tablet under those other ten things.

Prevention Is Impossible

Several years ago I had a small assignment with a provider of military weapons systems. The task was to participate as a team member in helping management identify some areas of waste that could be mined for profit. We used several methods to highlight savings potential, one of them being the cost of quality. The cost of quality is a proven technique of measuring the costs associated with MEDs. During the discussion, I asked the group to estimate the cost of waste on a single operation that was involved in assembling the weapon system. They were to begin by estimating what the cost of assembly would be if there were no MEDs.

At least two of the participants threw up their hands and argued that prevention was impossible. They explained how complex this product was. They argued that the unit was very high-tech and could not be expected to be without MEDs. Then they used one of my all time favorites: "This operation involves people. People cannot be expected to do tasks error free."

I asked them if they had ever assembled one unit without a MED. They said, "Yes." Then I asked them if they had ever assembled ten in a row without a MED. Again they responded, "Yes." I asked about twenty in a row? They conferred and again said, "Yes."

"If you can build twenty consecutive assembles without errors, why not twenty-five or fifty or a hundred?" I asked. "What made these twenty right? What did you do on each of them that produced an error-free assembly? The problem is that you that do not believe that you can make all of them right. You expect some to be wrong. Don't you see? This is a self-fulfilling prophecy. You 'know' in your own mind that they cannot be built correctly. You communicate this to everyone involved by the example of what you do when one is bad. Everyone knows that no one is expected to do things right. So they don't. I would recommend that you change your belief and then act according to your new belief, act to find what went wrong, and pursue the cause until it is permanently prevented. If you change your belief and then take actions that support your new belief, the message that things can be done like they were planned will flow through the organization.

"If you are to change this situation you must believe that the job can be done right the first time. Then you must expect people to do it right every time."

I doubt that I changed their minds. They had decades to develop these beliefs. I suspect the whole organization believed the same thing. If the others had not believed things could not be done correctly, there would have been some efforts within the organization to change these peoples' minds. I know that when management insists that the organization focus on prevention and error-free performance, things change for the better.

The Timing Isn't Right

Timing is very important; just ask any comedian. We all have things to do without adding another initiative. But just consider: If your organization is only halfway to my estimate of the potential savings (that is, 15 percent instead of 30 percent), every week you delay costs you dearly. Getting started is difficult, but to begin you must take that first step.

The best way to measure the results of prevention is to express it in terms that are familiar to management and captures its attention.

Made-up measures and indexes, regardless of their logic, do not work as well. Let me tell you a story.

Quality Vulnerability Index

At Datapoint Corporation in the mid-1970s, it was routine for John Walker, VP of operations, to hold a Project Operations Review every two weeks. During this meeting, we would cover the performance of the operations of the company. A typical meeting lasted all afternoon and involved reports from each operating organization: Customer Service, Sales, Project Management, and anyone else John invited to participate. A typical meeting would have about forty attendees shoehorned into a small conference room in the main manufacturing facility. Johnny's boss, Harold O'Kelley, usually attended. Harold was the chairman, CEO, and anything else he wanted to be.

It was not unusual for these meeting to involve some strong emotions. The old story was that after the meeting started, the first to bleed would be attacked and dismembered by the circling sharks. None of us wanted to be the first to bleed, or even to bleed at all, for obvious reasons.

I had come to Datapoint from LTV Aerospace. When I joined Datapoint, I discovered the company did not have a system for routinely reporting the problems that were occurring in the factory. Without reliable information, we were constantly surprised by rework, warranty costs, missed schedules, and the like. This environment created a reliance on reacting to problems as they surprised us. It had bred a culture within Datapoint of "all hands on deck." The company was young, and everyone knew that, at any time, we could be asked to inspect, pack, drive the forklift, or do anything else it took to keep things flowing. This included days, nights, weekends, and holidays. Keeping the plant running was everyone's primary objective. Everyone was part of the team. It did not matter that you were in Engineering, Materials, Quality, or Service. When we had a problem, it was our problem. We all pitched in. We really needed a quality information system, and we needed it quickly.

Back at LTV, there was a young man, Mike Young, who had helped install a quality-information system there. We had had good success with that system. It was obvious that the conceptual design of the system for Datapoint was going to be virtually the same as the one we had implemented at LTV. I brought Mike Young to Datapoint and asked him to do at Datapoint what we had done at LTV. He quickly had it up and running.

As director of quality, I was a routine part of the presentations during the Project Operations Meeting. I would present forty to sixty graphs showing defect and failure rates by product. These charts involved everything from cradle to grave, from receiving through installation in the field for the United States and for other countries. I was usually reporting on the performance of other departments, so I had to be diplomatic in the way I presented the information. I always tried to give the possible bleeder advanced notice of the information so that he or she could have a ready defense and action plan.

We had a formal corrective action system that provided routine status reports on problems that had been identified for action. One of the routine charts I would review in this meeting involved the status of these corrective actions. This subject was one that always drew a lot of interest from everyone, especially Mr. O'Kelley. If an individual had been assigned the responsibility for taking an action, it was a good idea for him or her to have taken that action by the time the meeting occurred or to have a very good story as to why it had not been done. This extra little bit of attention helped move the actions that were necessary to correct problems. Each meeting I would present a list of problems that had been solved since the last meeting.

At one meeting, Mr. O'Kelley said, "Larry, I'm happy to hear each meeting that we have solved several problems. But honestly, I don't see it. I look at the financials from last quarter and from last year and I don't see improvement on the cost side because of these corrective actions. The actions we're taking involve buying new test equipment, buying better, more expensive parts, and so on. This costs money. I'm not sure we're getting our money's worth from all this. I only have one question. I want to know if we *are* getting any better. By next meeting, I want a single measure that will show if we're improving or not. I just don't see it now."

Of course I assured him we could do that.

I had two weeks to come up with a single chart that would show our improvement. This was a very complex task. We had a whole series of hardware models: some simple, some complex. We had mechanical devices like printers and large washing machine-size hard drives. It would not be easy to make this happen on a single sheet of paper. But I had one advantage. I knew that Harold was an engineer, I was a mathematician, and that we both understood numbers.

I kicked the idea about with some associates and decided that we needed a common measure of the complexity of each device we delivered. I observed that simple terminals had relatively few components mounted on relatively few circuit boards. Each component on the board had leads that had to be soldered. If I could estimate the number of operations necessary to produce a shippable unit, I could have a relative measure of the chance for mistakes, errors, and defects to occur. The more components, the more solder joints, and the more assembly required resulted in a greater chance that something would go wrong. I called this chance of something going wrong "the vulnerability of the shippable unit." The fewer things that had to be done to manufacture a shippable unit, the lower was the vulnerability. Once I had the estimated vulnerabilities of the product-delivery mix, I could do a weighted average and, voila! I would have a measure of the vulnerability of the products shipped in a selected period of time. Then I would simply count the number of mistakes, errors, and defects, divide by the total vulnerability of the items shipped, and we would have a quality vulnerability index (QVI). I could see it now: a paper at the annual ASQC convention.

The anticipated meeting date arrived, and I was ready. When my time came, I proudly moved to the projector and quickly took the group through the logic of the QVI. I explained that it was a crude estimate but that we would refine over the next month. The room was quiet. Obviously they were stunned by the sheer brilliance of this approach. I continued to explain that it was obvious that we had improved for each of the last four quarters. I was happy to show the latest quarter had a QVI of eighteen point seven times ten to the minus sixth power.

Mr. O'Kelley broke the silence. "I have one question. What does a QVI of eighteen point seven times ten to the minus sixth power mean? How does it relate to anything, to the out-of-box failure rate, the schedule-misses, the cost of doing business, to anything? Just anything?"

I stammered, "Well it's the number of defects divided by the weighted average of the estimated vulnerabilities of—"

Harold interrupted, "I don't understand it at all. What I want is a simple answer to the question I asked two weeks ago. Are we better or not?! Are our costs lower?"

It would serve no purpose to continue with the rest of the story. Just let it be said that I had gotten a lesson in measurement, information, and management communication all rolled into one. Needless to say, at the next meeting I did not present the QVI.

Real improvements that are made within an organization must have a tangible impact on the organization's performance. The best measure of results is bottom-line financial impact.

Conclusion

Before we end this discussion about prevention, let's revisit Juan and Rita and the Casa Solana case. This case is intended to illustrate the pervasive nature of MEDs in our day-to-day experience. In the case of Juan and Rita, MEDs cost them time and money. It caused unnecessary trips to and from Atlanta resulting in lost days of work, not to mention that they did not have the use of the condo for several weeks. Of course, it was an emotional drain as well. The developer, sales group, and contractors also spent extra time and money redoing things that should have been done correctly the first time. In this case, the impact of these MEDs remains unmeasured and therefore largely unrecognized.

It is obvious that the Casa Solana organizations responsible to sell, prepare, and transfer ownership of the condo had problems. If they had understood the elements of the Ladder, they would have learned from the experience of other similar projects and would have adjusted that knowledge based on the current situation. From this knowledge they could have installed aids to help their associates do it right. It would have saved everyone a lot of time, money, energy, and emotion.

It cannot go without being noted that those responsible for the management of these processes were absent when things did not go as expected. The associates on the front line, facing the customers, suffered the ire of customers in this situation. The front-office staff appeared to be positive, well intentioned, and helpful, but they could not get the job done as expected. They had neither the understanding nor the systems they needed to do the job right the first time. The players were positive and willing, but management had chosen not to provide an environment and the support systems that would allow them to be successful. They were just doing business as usual. In this situation, there are no winners. Everyone loses.

Through this example, we see that a lot of things can go wrong. It seems no one or no organization is exempt from the trouble and waste caused by MEDs. Fortunately, MEDs are caused by mechanisms that can be largely eliminated from the processes that make up human endeavor. The process for the elimination of these MEDs is understood and can be implemented in any organization, if that organization's management has the will, courage, and persistence to make it happen.

The Prevention Ladder depicts the elements of a prevention process that can be used to greatly reduce the incidence and severity of the MEDs in any organization. When implemented, prevention can change the face of business as we know it. With this changed face comes the savings that accrue as a result of not wasting time and resources making up for things that have not gone as planned. As previously mentioned, my experience has shown that 30 percent of a typical organization's operating costs can be recovered. With appropriate management focus and emphasis, half of this is recoverable within two years. The Prevention Ladder provides a road map for an executive team that wants to lead its organization to prevention.

The recommended approach, implementation of the elements of the Ladder, does not require that the improvement efforts start from scratch, nor does it require that the organization throw out functioning systems installed as part of a previous improvement initiative. Instead, these systems become elements in the implementation of the Ladder.

It is true that following this approach requires constant management attention and commitment, but so do accounting and sales. With the necessary prevention systems in place, however, routine habitual prevention becomes significantly simpler. With this comes the benefit of living in an environment that is less hectic and more profitable, and one in which you will be able to cash the prevention check.

Index

978-0-595-35973-8
0-595-35973-6

www.ingramcontent.com/pod-product-compliance
Lightning Source LLC
Chambersburg PA
CBHW030839180526
45163CB00004B/1384